"Two-thirds of US small businesses have one owner, one employee. About 52 percent are home-based. This is a book of sound, logic-driven advice aimed directly at them."
—Ray Hoffman
CEO Radio, WCBS Newsradio 880

"As an entrepreneur and someone who works with attorneys, I may have a unique perspective on the importance of planning for your business's success. In Mitch and Barry's book, you'll learn exactly how to protect yourself and avoid the mistakes and missteps that other business owners fail to recognize until it's too late."
—Steve Fretzin
Three-Time Author & Legal Business Development Coach

"This is the book I wish I had before starting my business. There are 3 sides to every story – yours, theirs, and the truth. This book will help you make sure there is only one story if an issue comes up in your business."
—Jason Cutter
CEO, Cutter Consulting Group. Author of *Selling With Authentic Persuasion: Transform from Order Taker to Quota Breaker*

"Having worked with over 1,000 small business owners one-on-one, I have encountered many legal challenges that the business owners could have easily avoided had they employed the valuable knowledge outlined in this book. Mitch does an excellent job of breaking down common legal pitfalls to avoid and how to do it."
—Andrew Frazier, MBA, CFA/Business Growth Pro & CFO/Founder, Small Business Pro University

"Unlike other legal texts for entrepreneurs, Mitchell Beinhaker and Barry Cohen provide concrete advice that can actually be used by readers as they plan and operate their business enterprises. Not only do they tell readers the risks that can haunt them but also how to be proactive to avoid them and best ensure success."
—Douglas J. Wood, Esq, Reed-Smith

10 Ways To Get Sued By Anyone And Everyone

The Small Business Owner's Guide To Staying Out Of Court

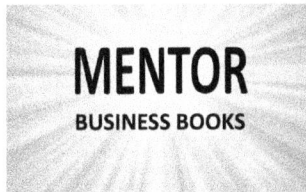

MENTOR

BUSINESS BOOKS

Habent Sua Fata Libelli

MENTOR
BUSINESS BOOKS

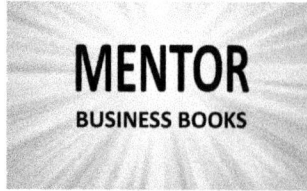

Manhanset House
Shelter Island Hts., New York 11965-0342

bricktower@aol.com • tech@absolutelyamazingebooks.com
• absolutelyamazingebooks.com
The Mentor Business Books is a joint imprint of Absolutely Amazing eBooks
and AdLab Media Communications, LLC.
The Absolutely Amazing eBooks colophon is a trademark of
J. T. Colby & Company, Inc.

Library of Congress Cataloging-in-Publication Data
Beinhaker, Mitchell C.
Cohen, Barry H.
10 Ways To Get Sued By Anyone And Everyone.
p. cm.
1. LAW / Practical Guides.
2. LAW / Business & Financial.
3. BUSINESS & ECONOMICS / Business Law.
Non-Fiction, I. Title.
ISBN: 978-1-955036-46-7 Trade Paper

July 2023

10 Ways To Get Sued By Anyone And Everyone

The Small Business Owner's Guide To Staying Out Of Court

Mitchell C. Beinhaker, Esq.
Barry H. Cohen

Also by the Authors

Mitchell C. Beinhaker

Podcast: "The Accidental Entrepreneur"

Barry H. Cohen

10 Ways to Screw Up an Ad Campaign
co-author of *Comin'Home,* a novel
Soul Switchers, a novel

Available from
AbsolutelyAmazingEbooks.com

Dedication
To all those brave entrepreneurs that risk it all.
Use this book to reduce your risk...

Disclaimer
This book is not intended to be a substitute for hiring your own competent legal counsel. Laws vary from state to state. This book serves as general guidance for business owners.

Table of Contents

Acknowledgments

Matthew Goerke. Matthew Goerke is regarded as one of America's leading experts in the field of Memory Development. He has shared with thousands of business professionals from all walks of life the techniques for developing an instant recall memory with results that can only be described as amazing. Matthew has worked with such well know speakers as Zig Zigler, Ed Forman, Vic Conant and Tony Robbins. He has trained executives from corporations including AT&T, Prudential, Exxon, Wells Fargo, Merck Pharmaceutical and Coldwell Banker, and government agencies such as the United States Postal Service and the Defense Department; 35 years in business; creator of "The Memory Switch";

http://www.memoryswitch.com/

Susan Reach Winters. Chiesa, Shahinian & Giantomasi, PC; Susan Reach Winters brings more than 35 years of experience across all areas of family law - including divorce, prenuptial agreements, business and other asset valuations, custody and timesharing, child support, alimony and equitable distribution. Widely regarded among the region's foremost thought leaders on family law, Susan recently authored *That Will Never Happen to Us*, which provides tips, strategies and other insight into the gamut of financial, emotional and familial considerations that must go into a successful and lasting relationship.; 35+ years in practice; honors include *The National Law Journal*, Family/Elder Law Trailblazers (2022),

Chambers High Net Worth, Family/Matrimonial Law: New Jersey - Band 1 & 2 (2021-2022), *Morris/Essex Health & Life Magazine*, Top Lawyers, Family Law (2021-2022). CIANJ Enterprising Women in Commerce, Law Industry Award (2021);

https://www.csglaw.com/biographies/susan-reach-winters

Harvey Topitz. Rivers Insurance Group; Harvey Topitz has 30 years in the insurance industry. At Liberty Mutual, he was named to the Top Producer Club. At BRI he introduced innovating services such as an asbestos abatement program. While with Tanenbaum-Harbor, now T&H Brokers, he excelled in the hard-to-insure employee leasing industry (PEO) and the entertainment sector, insuring such talents as Eminem, 50 Cent, Taking Back Sunday and Slipknot. Current clients in the entertainment sector include Bobby Ray Simmons, aka B.o.B. and Lupe Fiasco.;

http://www.ri-gi.com/

Andrew Botwin. SPC Consulting; Andy has extensive experience in public accounting, both as an auditor and Chief Human Resources Officer. Andy has worked for a top 10 national staffing and payroll agency gaining experience in recruiting, payroll, and risk management. Andy brings a unique blend of services including executive coaching, workplace culture consulting, training, and independent workplace investigations in EEO matters together in his practice. Andy has successfully worked with many levels of leaders from small entrepreneurial businesses to Fortune 100 companies; 15 years in practice; recognized on *Fortune Magazine's* 100 Best Places to Work in America for an organization;

http://www.strategypeopleculture.com/

Damien Weinstein. Weinstein & Klein, PC; Damien Weinstein counsels clients throughout the employment cycle – from hiring to firing, everyday compliance, and managing employee relations. Damien also has more than 10 years of litigation experience – something that helps him shape a plan and strategy for all of his clients; 11 years in practice; *SuperLawyers* Rising Star (2018-present);

http://www.weinsteinklein.com/

Steven Mitnick. SM Law PC; Steven Mitnick is an attorney and founder of SM Law PC where he specializes in business insolvency and liquidations and debt collection. Over the course of his 40 years in the industry, Mr. Mitnick has personally handled more than 300 assignments for the benefit of creditors proceedings as well as receivership actions and all forms of corporate wind downs. His clients include bankruptcy trustees, assignees and receivers and he has served as a court appointed Chapter 11 trustee, receiver, special fiscal agent, and as an assignee for the benefit of creditors in numerous federal and state court insolvency proceedings; 41 years in practice;

http://sm-lawpc.com/

Jon Bender. Jonathan L. Bender, P.C.; Jonathan (Jon) Bender concentrates his legal practice on accounts receivable litigation. Jon is the author of several eBooks on legal collections, including *Collecting After a Sale of Goods: The New Jersey Supplier's Guide to Getting Paid Quickly* (available for free download on his website). Jon lives with his wife and 4 children in Cherry Hill; 26 years in practice;

http://www.b2bcollectionlaw.com/

Joann Seery. Serious Business Solutions, Inc.; Joann A. Seery, MBA, is an accomplished dynamic consultant with an entrepreneurial spirit. Since 1998 Joann has helped entrepreneurs by writing business plans for new and existing businesses. The business plan helps to advise businesses on strategic business decisions through reviewing these plans for efficient and profitable operations.; 24 years in business; recognized as SBA Women in Business Champion for the State of Hawaii – 2008 • SBA Women in Business Champion Honolulu County – 2006 • Top SBA Technical Assistant Provider for State of Hawaii – 2006;

https://seriousbusinesssolutions.info/

Robert Drolet. Bailey Duquette P.C.; Robert manages Intellectual Property matters in the United States and internationally. He actively manages Patent, Trademark, and Copyright portfolios for domestic and international clients. Robert, also litigates intellectual property issues in Federal Court; 6 years in practice, https://www.baileyduquette.com/robert-drolet

Edward Altabet. Cohen, Seglias, Pallas, Greenhall & Furman, P.C.; Ed is an experienced litigator who counsels businesses and entrepreneurs across a broad range of industries including financial services, banking, wealth management, technology, manufacturing, export/import, construction, and real estate. Clients trust him to help them resolve their commercial and civil disputes involving contracts, lenders' and creditors' rights, secured transactions, real property, distressed businesses, securities, partnership disputes, business torts, and executive employment issues. He also represents companies, not-for-profit corporations, religious institutions, and directors and senior executives in connection with corporate governance matters, including internal and regulatory-driven investigations relating to allegations of financial misconduct and breaches of fiduciary duties;
https://www.cohenseglias.com/

Mark Greenberg. Mark Greenberg is the President of Breakthrough Mediation. He has tried over 100 cases to verdict, representing both Plaintiffs and Defendants in state and federal court. He now mediates cases throughout Florida, saving clients over $25 million dollars in legal expenses during 2021, while helping them find peace in the resolution of contentious disputes; 27 years in practice;
https://www.btmediation.com/

Foreword

When I was asked to write a Forward for *10 Ways to Get Sued by Anyone and Everyone*, my first reaction was, "OK. This will probably be like all the other legal advice books I've read that are used to solicit clients rather than impart valuable advice." To put it mildly, I was wrong. Unlike other legal texts for entrepreneurs, Mitchell Beinhaker and Barry Cohen provide concrete advice that can actually be used by readers as they plan and operate their business enterprises. Readers will be prepared to have intelligent conversations not with just their lawyers, but also their bankers, insurance agents, real estate brokers and more. This book arms them with what they need to know. Their examples are invaluable. The experts they consulted provide real life stories that help make the theoretical, reality. Not only do they tell readers the risks that can haunt them but also how to be proactive to avoid them and best ensure success. And they do it in a way that avoids legalese!

In the nearly fifty years I've practiced law, I've been amazed time and time again how the most sophisticated and educated clients I had could be so blind to taking simple steps to protect their businesses, themselves, their families, their employees, and their clients and suppliers. And, more importantly, how they do so little planning to avoid audits and lawsuits that often end in bankruptcy or divorce (of both business partners and spouses). It took me years to realize that business people, particularly entrepreneurs, are driven and rarely let anything or anyone get in the way, including lawyers. They abhor any negative thinking, a false trait they see in lawyers. So they avoid them. As Messrs. Beinhaker and Cohen show, doing so is a recipe for failure.

One of the most common quotes of Shakespeare is from the *Merchant of Venice*. "The first thing we do, let's kill all the lawyers." No doubt many entrepreneurs and small business owners identify with that sentiment. But the missing lesson in the Bard's play is the reason the character, Dick the Butcher, said those words. By killing all the lawyers, he wanted to eliminate the rule of law and be free to secure the illegal fruits of his criminal enterprise. In truth, Shakespeare saw lawyers as pillars in an orderly society. Readers of both William Shakespeare and Mitchell Beinhaker and Barry Cohen could learn a thing or two on the importance of making lawyers your partner and not your antagonist.

This book is a primer every business owner needs to read and take to heart.

—Douglas J. Wood, Esq, Reed-Smith

Introduction

As a co-author of this book, along with my good friend Barry, my goal is to provide valuable and   educational information to individuals and business owners to help them avoid common mistakes that people make when they try to do things on their own or seek advice from the wrong person or persons. Your Uncle Sol, the real estate lawyer, may not have any experience with corporate contracts. At the risk of insulting him, politely decline his offer to help. That also goes for Jimmy, your nephew in his second year of law school. Although he is well intentioned, consider that he just doesn't have the necessary real-world experience to help you navigate the choppy waters of entrepreneurship yet. Why let him learn at your expense?

Most important, when you "do things on your own", without the advice and counsel of a competent professional, you often do not know the problems you are creating and the issues you may face until it is too late. It is when the contract dispute arises or death of a partner occurs, that it is too late to correct those issues. Proper documentation before you open your doors to conduct business lays the groundwork or, rather, "sets the rules" for parties to abide by if disputes or other situations arise. And you set these rules when parties are in agreement, partners are all alive and well, etc... And it takes a professional with years of experience to recognize issues and protect clients from things you may not even be aware of due to your own lack of experience. I hope you find the information herein to be helpful and enlightening.

Chapter One
Creating Business Agreements by Yourself

This is truly the number one way for your business to end up with a lawsuit. If you think you're saving money by creating your own agreements, consider the cost of defending a lawsuit. I think you will agree that an ounce of prevention is worth a pound of cure, as the old adage goes. Over the years, I have reviewed countless agreements and contracts written by business owners and lay people (even those who have graduated from law school!) that fall short of doing anything beyond describing a relationship or transaction between the parties. I've never read one that was sufficient to protect the parties and to cover those frequently occurring business issues that face nearly every fledgling business (and please know that I rarely make definitive statements).

Contracts are written to protect all parties in the event that the relationship goes awry, steers off course, or if there is a misunderstanding between people. All these contracts must contain a process or mechanism for handling these disputes and making it clear that this written contract embodies their entire agreement and understanding. Often, as parties work together, they say things and make verbal commitments that may "change" their relationship. If they agree in writing that any oral agreements are not binding, it will avoid a lot of miscommunications (and potential legal actions.) In general, lay people have not had enough experience with various agreements and transactions to anticipate or even address these issues in a contract. When it comes to the law and contracts, it always comes down to the question: what was the intent of the parties?

Let's examine some of the common issues or elements that should be addressed in most of your agreements. Obviously, the date, names of the parties to the contract and their addresses should be stated at the beginning of the agreement (you'd be surprised what people leave out!). Other provisions should address the term (time length) of the agreement, obligations of the parties (depending on what the document is for), how to resolve disputes or disagreements, voting rights, what state law applies and where suits should be filed (those might be different), and that all understandings of the parties are limited to the agreement and only can be changed in writing. This last statement is important – more often than not people believe that their emails, text messages, letters, etc… can be used to "create" a contract if needed. While that may be possible, it is extremely difficult since you really do not know what was agreed upon and the door is open for a lot of "he said, she said," misunderstandings, misinterpretations and just differing in memory. Minds are fallible and parties tend to remember their dealings very differently – even with honest people; it's just human nature. Here is a real-world example of how this occurs.

An investor knew of a local restaurant owner that was looking to raise or borrow money to improve his business. The investor reviewed the owner's financial statements and concluded that he would privately loan the business money with the ability to convert some or all of the debt to ownership in the business. The parties drafted their own agreement, and the restauranteur later ran into trouble keeping up with payments. Over time, the investor made many concessions: extending payment dates, terms, etc… In return, the owner (supposedly – important distinction) made additional promises to pay higher interest and offer additional equity. Eventually, the relationship soured as the business owner got farther and farther behind in payments and eventually defaulted on the agreement. The investor sought legal assistance to collect his money, something the investor believed was fairly straightforward. At the end of the day, there was so much back and forth, verbal promises (not in writing) and misunderstandings, that the situation erupted in protracted and costly litigation. The investor had to settle for a lesser amount, paid over time and was not reimbursed for his legal fees. (A legal fee provision is another essential part of all good contracts.) If you think you can rely on memory—yours and the other party's, think again. See what our memory expert has to say in the sidebar.

SIDEBAR
MEMORY, IMPERFECT WITH A DEMAND FOR PERFECTION

As we've indicated, memory isn't always reliable and can't be depended upon when it comes to agreements between parties in a business situation—which leaves a wide-open door to disputes and to potential lawsuits. There is always your memory and the other party's memory, but they're usually not the same. For more insight into the subject, we consulted memory expert Matthew Goerke, creator of The Memory Switch™. *Take a look at the insights he provided into how the memory works—and how this might affect your future interactions in business.*

First of all, Matt makes a point in distinguishing between overall memory as opposed to *recall*. Recall is the critical component here. In no uncertain terms, Matt states that memory recall is very subjective. He muses about the trial lawyer questioning a witness about his or her police interview when they ask the person where they were on a specific date…four years ago.

When it comes to the law, the law treats you like you should be able to recall anything and everything—if not, you are either an idiot or you are lying! (Author's observation.) As a lawyer, that's why it's so easy to discredit a witness—you just confuse them during a deposition…and then at trial, ask them the same question and nail them when they give a different answer.

However, in Matt's words, "The memories still exist. The reality is people don't forget. They can't recall." Believe it or not, our memory expert says, "Placement of information is really key." You have to put it in a place where you can access it to recall it.

Let's take a different real-life scenario. When NBC news anchor Brian Williams said he was in the field as a war correspondent and claimed he had been shot down in a helicopter, he didn't intentionally lie or make up a story. He most likely became confused. He told what he *thought* was the truth. So, how reliable is the average person's memory?

Well, according to our expert, 85% of people will forget a person's name in the first *two minutes*. That said, why would you stake the future of your business dealings on the strength of anyone else's memory, let alone your own? So, how do you mitigate this effect? Well, Matthew advises the following: "First, slow down; next, focus; then repeat the information several times to yourself. Do this and you will find yourself in the top 15% of the population."

Author's advice. Follow Matt's advice and create a mental picture so you see the information AND THEN **WRITE IT DOWN.** Never do business on a handshake. Have all parties to an agreement sign off and date it. Written agreements are much more difficult to dispute than anyone's memory.

* * *

Advice #1 – Do NOT write your own agreements and do not think you have an agreement just because you believe you can prove your position through texts, emails or other correspondence.

Chapter Two
Not Having A Written Agreement With Your Partner(s)

Businesses with multiple partners (I use the term "partner" to include also members of an LLC and shareholders of a corporation), whether LLCs, corporations or partnerships, must be subject to written operating documents. Whether an operating agreement (LLCs), bylaws (corporations) or partnership agreements, these documents set the rules and regulations under which the business will operate— who has what powers, when you may or may not be personally liable, what occurs if a partner dies, what happens if the business gets sued, provisions for taking on new partners, dissolution of the company, etc. It should also include a section that sets rules for resolving any disputes that arise between partners of the business. While this agreement may be changed over time, it rarely is referred to until problems come about. And, unless you have the experience of writing many of these agreements for many different types of businesses, you will not be aware of all the provisions that should or can be included. A typical operating agreement or set of bylaws should include at the very least, along with all the standard provisions mentioned above, the powers of each partner, who is responsible for day-to-day operations, what issues need to be voted on, and what might happen if the business stops operating.

Ownership by Birthright?
Commonly in family situations, businesses are operated without bylaws or an operating agreement. Maybe the father or grandfather started the business, as the sole owner, and now a few children or other family members have taken over. As a case in point, a regional logistics company was owned, 50/50 by 2 brothers. At the outset of the

business, they were both equally active and the business was doing a few million dollars in revenue each year. Over the years, the business grew to $80 million (yes, million!) in annual sales. The main brother, now the president, ran the company, brought in most of their business, and the other brother just took his check (salary and profits) and didn't do much anymore. He rarely showed up to work and even when given projects and responsibilities, he didn't see them through. How does the main working brother convince the other that he should own a larger share, receive a larger portion of the profits and control the general decision-making? Most of the time, the other brother stayed out of things, but for certain issues they both needed to vote. The only "agreement" that existed was their history of handling the business together. The working brother had put himself in a precarious position in that his lazy sibling really had the upper hand. He did not have to sign anything or agree to any changes in the business. A suit between the parties would, at best, lead to a "partition" where the court orders the business be split up and sold. This situation has occurred with many similar businesses throughout the country.

Although your basic operating documents may address how to handle a partner's death, they do not deal with the issue of how to treat surviving heirs. Do they get bought out? Are they entitled to take over the decedent's shares in the company and now participate in running the business? What if a partner becomes disabled and cannot return to work? How long do you have to continue to pay him or her? Or can you force a buyout? These issues, along with retirement and "involuntary" transfers (creditors and divorce, mostly), should be addressed in a separate document called a "buy-sell" agreement. You may not need it at the outset of the business, but you should get something in place soon thereafter. You can also consider "funding" the agreement with life insurance or other financial products to help the surviving partners better deal with these crises.

SIDEBAR
YOUR WORST LAWSUIT NIGHTMARE—YOUR SPOUSE

Business owners beware. You may not have considered how serious this scenario could be – – worse than your business partner, your clients or your supplier suing you – – if you own a business, know that a divorce is probably going to be your worst lawsuit nightmare. We consulted one of the most knowledgeable professionals on the subject, Susan Reach Winters, Esq. She literally wrote the book! She was an author of one of the original treatises on family law in the State of New Jersey and is the author of *That Will Never Happen To Us, a divorce lawyer's guide for couples getting married – and their parents, too!* Susan practices family law in New Jersey, New York, and Florida. Heed her advice and seek competent counsel to protect the business you have built.

In most states, the value of a business started during the marriage is a marital asset subject to being shared with your spouse in a divorce. Even if the business was started prior to your marriage, the increase in the *value* of the business due to your efforts may be subject to being shared with your spouse. This is the case even if your spouse never actually assisted you in running your business. So, how can a business owner protect his or her assets and income from the divorcing spouse? Well, according to our expert, unfortunately there is very little one can do to protect oneself. Her best suggestion is to have a prenuptial agreement (or "prenup") or put assets, including your business, into a trust. Better yet – – her preferred scenario to protect your business involves layering the prenup with a trust. There is specific language that should be in the prenup and the trust to make sure it is not accessible to your

17

spouse. Your best bet is to consult with both a family law attorney and a trusts and estates attorney in this regard to eliminate your spouse from becoming the biggest creditor in your life. Your worst nightmare is that your spouse becomes your business's creditor in a divorce.

If you have a prenup that specifically excludes your business as a marital asset, you obviously want to also exclude any appreciation or increase in the value of that business, even if it is due to your active participation in the business during the marriage. Too often, business owners are of the mistaken belief that because they owned the business prior to the marriage it would not be considered a marital asset. However, in New Jersey and other states, the increase in the *value* of the premarital business during the marriage, based on one's activities, even if peripherally so, could result in the increase in value of the premarital business being considered a marital asset without a prenup. In some states, a very lenient interpretation of "active in a business" is applied. For example, you might be retired but day trading your own account and your spouse can claim that it is your "business" and demand a piece of the "value" of that business in addition to a share of the assets in your trading account.

You also want the prenup to specifically state that even if your spouse somehow financially or otherwise contributes to the business during the marriage, he or she is still not entitled to a share of it in a divorce. The bottom line is that there's just no way to avoid your business or the increase in value of your business from being included in the marital estate unless you specifically exclude it by way of a prenup and/or a trust. Even if you do not own a business at the time you are getting married, the prenup /trust should exclude any future business that you may start during the marriage if it is your intention to do so in the future.

In the best of both worlds, marrying couples should be able to talk about a prenup and be able to convey their feelings as to their concept of marriage from a financial standpoint, including one's interest in the other one's business. What other partnership would you ever enter into without a written agreement that spells out what happens if one of the partners wants out, or if one of the partners dies? A prenup is just like a business plan or an operating agreement—which of course you would have in connection with your business. It sets up the rules for the business in the event that the business owner dies or gets divorced. And, of course, you are entering into a prenup when you are happily engaged rather than when you are getting divorced, and emotions are strained.

Often times in a second marriage, the business owner wants to gift/ leave the business to his children and a prenup/trust can take care of that. Otherwise, the second wife and the spouse's children will be adversaries in a lawsuit post the death of the business owner. This can be avoided by specifically excluding the business in a prenup/trust so that it can be freely gifted during the marriage or bequeathed upon the business owner's death. The prenup should include a waiver of the right of election by the second spouse. It is a good suggestion to provide some financial consideration to the second wife for this waiver, such as a substantial life insurance policy with her as beneficiary. (Author's note: The genders may in fact be reversed if the wife is the primary business owner.)

A problem that often occurs in divorce is that one spouse claims the prenup is not enforceable. To be enforceable, one requirement is that you need to have full disclosure of your assets, liabilities and income. When you enter into a prenup, most people do not have their business interest actually valued because they don't want to go through the expense. Instead, they include an estimated value for their business which the other spouse then tries to use as a means to invalidate the prenup in the future, claiming that the business was undervalued. A provision in the prenup acknowledging that the business value is an estimate and that it is acceptable nonetheless and agreeing that the non-business owner spouse will not use the fact that the business was not valued properly as a means to invalidate the prenup will guard against your spouse being able to do so in the future.

"Best advice: enter into a prenup, put it in a safe deposit box and never think about it again!"

The worst prenup is one that automatically terminates after a certain number of years. It is better to include a provision permitting a revision of its terms in the future if the spouses agree. The best advice: enter into a prenup, put it in your safe deposit box, and never think about it again!

Every contract is challengeable, subject to the particular facts and circumstances, including a prenup, which is never "iron-clad". In every case however, it is better to have one then not have one and, if prepared properly in accordance with the state's laws, as most modern prenups are, it will be enforceable. Even with a prenup, some spouses will receive advice from their lawyers to challenge it anyway in the hopes of squeezing something "more" from their spouse.

While none of us has a crystal ball that really works, and we don't know what the future holds, what do you do if you did not enter into a prenuptial agreement at the time you were getting married but now you want one? You can consider entering into a post nuptial agreement, which, as you can imagine is not the easiest thing to broach with your spouse. Be aware that many state courts have not been enthusiastic about enforcing post nuptial agreements, including New Jersey. Ms. Winters, relates that she is a "big fan" of two adults, even if they are married, being able to voluntarily contract for anything they want to. Like a prenuptial agreement, it will be invalidated if it is signed under duress. Many spouses claim a postnup was signed under duress because their spouses threatened them with divorce if they did not sign. While, of course, the choice to stay married or get divorced can be freely made, to guard against this claim, consider offering your spouse some financial consideration to enter into a postnup. That way, if the postnup is challenged, the spouse looking to enforce it can point to some monetary consideration that the other spouse received in exchange for whatever he/she waived in the postnup. Also, like a prenup, a postnup cannot be unconscionable which, unfortunately, is a subjective term, subject to wide interpretation.

So, what happens if you are a business owner involved in a divorce? Unfortunately, there are only three options:

1. Sell the business to a third-party.
2. "Buy out" your spouse's interest in the business; or
3. Have your spouse "ride along" as an "actual" or "constructive" partner.

Assuming you do not want to sell your business, if you have to buy out your spouse's interest you will have to engage a forensic accountant to determine the value of the business. If it is a business you owned prior to the marriage you will need to determine the value as of the date of the marriage and as of the date of the divorce complaint to ascertain the increase in value during the marriage. Either way, it costs a fortune. Not to mention, it is very disruptive to the business. What business owner ever wants his business gone through with a fine-tooth comb by a forensic accountant? And where does the money come from to buy out the non-business owner spouse? Often, the business owner spouse is forced to turn over other marital assets to the non-business owner spouse for his or her share of the value of the business. For some couples, the business value is their biggest asset, and they have little to no liquidity in their marital estate. In those cases, the business owner spouse will have to make payments over a period of time with interest—a double whammy!

More and more, spouses are opting to "ride along" because they think that the company is going to go public, or some other grand event is going to take place and they don't want to get bought out at the time of the divorce. They are counting on the business having a greater value in the future when there is such an event. In the meantime, they share in the profits and distributions, so they receive "mailbox money"! Some spouses would rather have that than the marital home or other fixed assets.

But, for the business owning spouse, it can be a nightmare for him and his partners to have the ex-spouse as a "partner" in the business after the divorce. How does one protect himself when entering into business with partners, in anticipation of a possible divorce down the road? One thing to do is to have a partnership agreement that specifically prohibits a partner's spouse from ever being able to be assigned an actual interest in the partnership. In that way, the ex-spouse will not be able to control anything in the business or be involved in any way post-divorce. The business owner spouse is in a very good position vis-à-vis the divorce court because he can point to the terms of the partnership agreement that restricts the spouse from becoming a partner.

If the ex-spouse cannot be an actual partner, but wants to ride along anyway, the same can be accomplished by a "constructive trust". The business owner takes on the role of a fiduciary and from his profits, distributions or proceeds of sale would provide the ex -spouse with her percentage thereof. (Note that same will be taxed at the business owner's tax rate given that he holds the actual ownership interest, which could be a negative to the ex-spouse if the business owner is in a much higher tax bracket.) If you are getting divorced and your spouse owns a business, you are really making a decision to invest in that business in the future or get bought out of it at the time out of the divorce. That decision should be made with the assistance of a financial advisor who is going to help you determine whether it makes sense financially to ride along because of future upside potential or take your money and run because the business is too risky!

If you are a business owner and you have an adult child, you definitely want to set up a trust or encourage that adult child to have a prenup that protects the business if you want to gift or bequeath it to the child. Without that, if your child receives that gift/bequest and works in the business during his marriage, his spouse will have a claim to the business that you spent your whole life building! While you can't anticipate every possible future scenario, seeking the advice of good counsel is the wisest course to protect your business.

*   *   *

Advice #2 – Don't run your business without having all the rules and regulations agreed upon and in writing ahead of time.

Chapter Three
No Contracts With Vendors, Suppliers Or Subcontractors

You might as well put out a sign on your front door saying, "sue me" (or "steal from me"), because you are inviting a plethora of potential lawsuits if you conduct business this way—more than you can ever imagine. Dealing with these types of individuals during the ongoing operation of your business is often difficult. Relationships lead to doing business "in the normal course" and transactions are subject to purchase orders or, in many cases, just a handshake. Sometimes purchase orders include small-print, boilerplate provisions on either the front or back of the order—provisions which you probably have not reviewed nor formally agreed to. It contains a clause, that by doing business and accepting their goods/services, you agree to the terms of the purchase order. This may include everything from delivery deadlines to payment due dates, to past due interest charges, to cancellation provisions. As a business owner, you are required to read what you "sign" and the courts have little sympathy for commercial businesses that don't.

If possible, you should provide your version of a contract to the vendor or subcontractor containing the provisions under which you are willing to do business. With subcontractors, you may have more control over this than with vendors or suppliers. If the other party insists on their provisions, you should at least take the time to read all provisions and obtain professional counsel to give you a legal opinion. A skilled attorney can help you create a standard agreement to use with these types of transactions. There are several "general provision" protective sections that should be included in most (if not all) of these types of contracts. Some provisions are as follows:

Complete Understanding of the Parties.

This Agreement constitutes the complete and exclusive statement of the understanding between the parties. It supersedes all prior written and oral statements, including any prior representation, statement, condition, or warranty. Except as expressly provided otherwise herein, this Agreement may not be amended without the written consent of both parties.

Waiver.

A waiver of any provision or provisions of this agreement by any authorized personnel does not and should not be construed as a waiver of all provisions of this agreement. In addition, each party reserves the right to revoke any such waiver at any time.

Changes or Modifications.

Unless expressly provided otherwise in this agreement, all waivers, requests, notices, consents, approvals, offers, acceptances, elections, certifications, objections or other official communications permitted or required by this agreement shall be in writing, duly signed by the person making the official act or request, and delivered personally, by courier, U.S. mail, or facsimile to the party receiving the writing at the then corporate headquarters of said party. Receipt shall be obtained by the sender for all deliveries.

Severability & Ambiguities.

Each provision of this Agreement shall be considered separable. And if for any reason, any provision or provisions herein are determined to be invalid and contrary to any existing or future law, such invalidity shall not impair the operation of or affect those portions of this Agreement which are valid. The Agreement has been drafted by [such and such Party] and, as such, any ambiguities shall not be construed against the drafter.

Headings (if any).

The headings herein are inserted as a matter of convenience only, and do not define or limit the scope of this Agreement or the intent of the provisions hereof.

Jurisdiction.

This agreement shall be governed by and subject to the laws of the State of _____.

Binding Agreement.

This agreement is binding upon all parties, their heirs, devisees, successors, legal representatives, and permitted assignees, but shall not be deemed to be for the benefit of creditors.

Attorneys Fees & Costs.

You agree, that in addition to your outstanding balance and interest, you will pay for all of our costs of collection including all legal costs, filing fees and any other costs of collection, related to the collecting of your unpaid balance.

Dispute Resolution.

Any controversy or claim, including both statutory and common law claims, arising out of or relating to this Agreement or the validity interpretation, enforceability or breach thereof, which is not settled by agreement between the parties, shall first be settled by non-binding mediation. If mediation is unsuccessful, such dispute(s) shall be settled by arbitration in accordance with the rules of the American Arbitration Association then in effect, and judgment upon the award rendered in such arbitration may be entered into any court having jurisdiction. The parties agree to use the expedited rules of the AAA including a hearing before one arbitrator to be held in the county of _____ in the State of _____. The parties hereby waive the jurisdictional limit of the expedited rules. The findings of any such arbitration shall be final, conclusive and binding upon the Parties, and may not be appealed to any court.

Depending on your trade or profession, associations sometimes provide industry-specific sample agreements for their members. Some industries have specific contracting requirements, especially if you are dealing with the general public. Commercial agreements might be just a guide, but in either case it can be a good source of information.

An example of a frequently occurring issue with contract language came up in the advertising industry. Advertising agencies represent the advertiser, not the media. However, on many occasions, advertisers paid their agencies who in turn, failed to pay the media. As a result, many media outlets adopted policies and contract language indicating that the advertiser and the agency were "jointly and severally liable" for payment. This also meant that if the advertiser failed to pay, the agency became liable for its client's bill. Advertising agencies typically only earn up to 15% commissions and felt that this unduly penalized them for ads that promoted the client's business, and not their own. The response from the agency community came in the form of a practice known as "in care of" billing, which specified that the advertiser and not the agency was liable in the event of non-payment. The agencies asserted "sequential liability"—meaning they were only liable to the extent that they were paid by the advertiser.

Douglas J. Wood, Esq, from the law firm of Reed Smith LLP is the author of the book *Please Be Ad-Vised,* published by the Association of National Advertisers (ANA) and has chaired the Global Advertising Lawyers Alliance (GALA). There appears to be no definitive case law on the sequential liability issue. Doug weighs in as follows:

"To my knowledge, there has never been a case that endorsed sequential liability. It's a concept that was invented by the 4A*'s when some brands went belly up leaving the agencies with massive media bills. So, the 4A's adopted sequential liability as a recommended policy and it found its way into most contracts. But media in general has never endorsed it and holds to the concept of joint and several liability, i.e., both parties are liable."

(*American Association of Advertising Agencies)

Even though using a well-written contract(s) is important to deal with disputes, misunderstandings, and bad actors, you may want to use some pre-emptive practices to minimize disputes overall.

If the situation allows, run credit and background checks before allowing a client or vendor to run up a balance. You can run D&B reports or get permission to pull credit reports from one of the three credit agencies (Experian®, TransUnion® and Equifax®).

Also, while you do not want to make it a habit nor announce this to customers, be flexible when it comes to extended payment plans. If someone or a company is going through tough times (rather than just avoiding their responsibility), receiving "slow" payments is much better than no payments at all along with the cost of delinquencies.

SIDE BAR
PROS & CONS OF USING COLLECTION AGENCIES

Collection problems are inevitable the longer you are in business and the more persons and companies you interact with. Just like bad tenants to the real estate owner, a client, customer or contractor who does not keep up with his or her obligations can be a difficult problem to deal with, one that may cost you money and disrupt your business. Below are some common pros and cons of using a collection agency to outsource your delinquent accounts.

The Pros

Potentially Successful and Faster Debt Recovery.
Going after unpaid accounts can be difficult but hiring a debt collection agency makes people pay their debts faster and more often. This is because debt collectors are experienced professionals trained to persuade debtors to pay.

Eliminate an uncomfortable confrontation with Customers.

Confronting customers about their overdue balances is not always comfortable, and no one loves the job of arguing with clients who refuse to pay. When you hire a collection agency, you free yourself from the unpleasant task, giving yourself time to focus on your business.

Debt collectors have tools and resources.

Agencies often have access to advanced skip-tracing technology to help locate debtors. Debt collection agencies may also report delinquent accounts to the credit reporting agencies, which may negatively affect a debtor's credit score. Debtors will often make arrangements to pay their debts to avoid damage to their credit.

Legal Protection.

Numerous federal and state laws govern the debt collection industry, and well-informed debtors won't hesitate to sue if they know a law has been broken. You should make sure your chosen collection agency is well-versed in these laws and rules for your state, as well as federal laws. Hiring a collection agency may mitigate the legal risks involved in trying to collect the debt on your own.

Shifting Focus Back to What Matters.

Letting a collection agency manage debt will allow you and your employees to focus on your core business activities instead of managing debt collection efforts.

Legal Assistance.

A collection agency can take care of everything for you. Filing a lawsuit to collect on a debt is just part of the collection process, but usually as a last resort. The collection agency may have an attorney who works with them or at least can assist the one you choose to hire. Additionally, with only around 80% of judgments being collected, a collection agency will know when it is practical to file a lawsuit.

The Cons

Debt Collectors Charge for Their Services.
The cost of employing a collection agency may be costly, ranging from 20% to as high as 45% of the amount collected. Be sure to negotiate the fee before you enter into any agreement with an agency.

Client Relations Could Be Affected.
Outsourcing to a debt collection agency can cause a negative reaction from any persons your business deals with and receiving a call from a collection agency can put a bad taste in a customer's mouth, especially if the agency lacks empathy skills. Therefore, your choice of agency is important.

While the pros and cons stated above are commonly written about, this specific information was reproduced, in part, from an article posted on thefaircapital.com. The entire article can be found at https://www.thefaircapital.com/post/pros-and-cons-of-hiring-a-debt-collection-agency. You can also do a search for "pros and cons of using a collection agency" to find similar articles.

Chapter Four
Failure To Purchase Various Types Of Liability Insurance

Big mistake! These include directors & officers (D&O), errors & omissions (E&O), employment practices (EPLI), and even cyber security coverage. While some types of insurance are expensive (and unavailable in certain circumstances and with certain industries), you should work with a skilled and knowledgeable insurance professional and an attorney who understands risk assessment and mitigation, so you at least know all of your options. There is nothing worse than facing a legal issue or claim and finding out later that you could have insured the business against this potential risk.

As in life, so in business—there will always be challenges. How well we prepare for them—and how we react to them determines how we succeed or fail. In our litigious society, there is always someone waiting around the corner looking to sue. So, how can we minimize our exposure to legal action? One of the best defenses we have is insurance. We spoke to Harvey Topitz of Rivers Insurance, a 39-year veteran of the risk management industry. While Harvey doesn't wear a superhero's cape—or a bulletproof vest for that matter, his advice can save you a great deal of hardship...as well as potentially, a great deal of money.

There are several key types of insurance that nearly every business should have. In addition, there are specialized policies for specialty businesses. We will enumerate the most important types of insurance and then explain them in detail. To wit, everyone in business should consider having the following commercial insurance policies:

General Liability
- Fire and theft
- Workers' Compensation (if you have employees)

- Employment Practices (if you have employees)
- Business Interruption
- Umbrella Protection

If you are a manufacturer or a distributor:
- Product Liability

If you are a professional corporation
(doctors, lawyers, accountants, etc):
- Professional Liability
(also knowns as errors and omissions, or E&O)
- Cyber Liability

If you have a board of directors:
- Directors and Officers (D&O)

Many businesses operate in rented facilities—whether you have a warehouse, a retail store or an office. If you don't own your commercial space, you still need insurance. As a tenant, most leases will require you to at least insure the contents of your business. As Harvey explains it, "If you were to turn the building upside down, everything that falls out—that's your contents." Conversely, that which is attached would be considered fixtures. Yes, the building owner needs to insure the property against hazards that can cause damage. However, what's inside is your responsibility. Fire and theft are covered under this policy provision.

But insuring the contents of your space is just the beginning. As a business owner in a rented space, you are responsible for maintaining a hazard-free, safe space, as well. You need to purchase a liability policy to protect you in the event someone (other than your employees) becomes injured on your premises. The landlord's policy will cover the grounds and the common areas of the facility, but once again—what happens in your space is your responsibility.

Pain and Gain
When it comes to general liability, think of two things: bodily injury and property damage. It's primarily for trips and falls. This coverage applies if you did damage to my body or to my property—for example,

you dropped paint on my car, or I walked into your office and I tripped over your poorly maintained carpet. There is also false arrest. If I come into your place and you accuse me of stealing and you hold me down, that's considered kidnapping so I could sue you for that. That's covered there. That's your basic package policy.

The cost of liability insurance is far less than the cost of defending a slip and fall suit, for example. Our expert advises you to purchase "all risk", rather than "named peril" coverage. You never know...while it's rare, lightning does strike. Keep in mind that water damage from a pipe bursting in the building that fries your computers may be covered but rising waters from the stream in the back that floods your office will <u>not</u> be covered—unless you purchase flood insurance from FEMA.

Suppose your building catches fire or the roof collapses and you can't continue your operation. Your clients have been promised delivery by a certain date and your facility is deemed uninhabitable. They might decide to sue your company for failure to meet the terms of your contract. However, you wisely purchased business interruption insurance that will help to cover your losses—or possibly pay the cost to relocate you to a temporary facility. This type of policy provision applies strictly to physical damage to your facility—not a business interruption caused by a pandemic, for example. As a result, insurance companies have often excluded bacteria and viruses.

Each state's insurance department governs its licensed carriers, and the companies will make every effort to secure approvals for their policy provisions. In every case, you must read the precise specific coverage you have. There will always be exclusions to every policy. Take note: insurance companies are smart. They have figured out nearly every possible contingency. They are in business to make money—not to lose money.

If you are a manufacturer, you will absolutely need to purchase product liability insurance. If a consumer buys your sunscreen and ends up with a severe skin rash, the lawsuits will start flying. Retail chain stores will not even place your product on the shelves if you don't produce proof of coverage—often policy limits to the tune of five million dollars or more of coverage. Remember the exploding batteries in the hoverboards kids were riding?

What is the definition of manufacturing? Suppose you didn't technically make the product, but you imported it and distributed it.

Same situation. The tequila you brought in from Mexico made someone sick and they filed a lawsuit. Unless you have adequate product liability insurance, you're on the hook for it. To quote Harvey Topitz directly, "Any time you bring something in over the water and there's no U.S. based company with US-based insurance, you're the manufacturer; you need product liability coverage." How technical does it get? Well, let's simplify it: any time you buy something in bulk, break it down, repackage and distribute it, you're the manufacturer, because the original manufacturer is going to say, they sent it to you clean—that's raw material.

Taking Care of Your People

Prior to 1970, the law only recognized workers compensation for work related accidents and injuries. As a result of the coal miners' union's lobbying efforts, Black Lung Disease crossed that threshold, followed by the textile workers' illness, known as brown lung disease. These two illnesses established the precedent that resulted in recognizing work related illnesses under the workers' compensation laws. If you employ people, you should purchase workers' compensation insurance to protect you against anyone claiming to suffer an injury or an illness related to their employment. For example, beyond the obvious, where a worker suffers from falling debris at a construction site, consider the risk posed by the person inhaling a noxious substance used in the performance of his or her daily routine. Your workers' compensation insurance will kick in when claims are filed, providing coverage for the ill or injured employee's related medical expenses.

While it's a more recent coverage category, employment practices policy provisions have become a standard. The cost is low; the limits are high, and the protection is well worth it, considering the sizeable judgments that the courts have handed down. We're talking about everything here from age, race and sex discrimination to sexual harassment, to wrongful termination suits.

There are both federal and state laws that apply to prohibited employment practices, so the wise choice is to not take them lightly. Of particular note, in the "me-too" era, people are especially sensitive to even the appearance of impropriety. The recent rash of high-profile figures in both the political and the entertainment worlds attest to this. The basic tenet here revolves around the concept of a "hostile work environment."

How do we define this? Well, it's anything from an employee making unwanted advances to another employee—regardless of their rank on the pecking order—to simply using foul language or posting lewd pictures in a work area. The key to what constitutes a hostile work environment: *if it makes an employee feel uncomfortable.*

Take it one step further. You are at your company picnic. George notices that Sally left her husband home and begins to flirt with her. She clearly is not interested. Even though it's not on company premises or during work hours, because it is a company function, it qualifies as a defensible event. Even the delivery man that keeps asking out your receptionist—and is not even your employee—can trigger a suit if you don't address her repeated requests to put a stop to the activity. Of course, management can't be held responsible until it becomes aware of the problem. Therefore, your response will determine whether your coverage will apply. Document all incidents that are reported to management. You have to notify the insurance company of the problem and what you are doing to remedy it. Most important, as our expert Harvey advises, be sure to have an employee handbook in everyone's hands when you apply for the coverage. And be sure to have all supervisors and managers familiarize themselves with it. It can help you dodge another bullet. As an example, a new employee at an insurance company needed to take a day off for a religious holiday during her probationary period. Her supervisor denied it; when they checked the employee handbook, it allowed for the absence. If you don't have an HR department or an HR Director, you can often purchase handbooks through payroll companies.

Beware the opportunist. Digital Forensics expert Rob Kleeger of Digital4nxGroup has often been called to "follow the breadcrumbs" in cases such as sexual harassment where a company may have a legitimate case against a disgruntled employee seeking to profit. By accessing the individual's computer, digital forensics experts have been able to track the employee's search history and support their intent to defraud or extort the company with a false claim of harassment.

HR consultant Andrew Botwin of Strategy-People-Culture would advocate that you invest in training your supervisors, managers and owners on issues such as discrimination and harassment as an extra measure of protection. This also provides additional documentation that the company has taken measures to avoid the issues that can result in lawsuits.

Although you would love to employ your whole family, if qualified applicants feel they were passed over because of their age, their gender or their race, they may well be inclined to sue. True, discrimination is hard to prove, but if they have a case, you may not only have to deal with a lawsuit, you might also find yourself mired in paperwork and an investigation from the Equal Employment Opportunity Commission (EEOC). And it's not just hiring or even firing. If an employee feels they were passed over for a promotion and it was because of discrimination— and they were in a protected class (ethnic minority, aged 40+, religious affiliation or even sexual orientation), they are inclined to sue. This is when your employment practices policy will kick in to defend you.

Protect Your Digital Assets

Prior to 2015, cyber liability coverage would hardly ever come up in conversation with your insurance agent. Today, having it is the wisest course. The critical issue is known as PII, or personally identifiable information. If you collect it and maintain it, you need to protect it. So, exactly what is PII? Someone's name, date of birth, social security number all qualify as PII. Back in the day, it was the stuff of spy movies—someone breaks into an office, cracks a safe and takes pictures of documents with a miniature camera. Today, it's far too easy to commit these crimes. Someone in another country can hack into your company's computers remotely and steal that information. Guess who is liable? You are.

Think about this. We all have some degree of exposure if we have anyone's PII, but certain types of businesses, especially professional practices have the most vulnerability. As a case in point, your accountant likely has your own information, your employees' information and your family members' information. In the wrong hands, without cyber liability coverage, you are courting disaster—a slew of lawsuits. What's even worse, cyber criminals can hold your data hostage with ransomware and other techniques.

Medical practices are extremely exposed to cybercrime. They not only have their patients' basic PII; they also have their confidential medical and health insurance information. You are responsible for securing that information. If it becomes compromised, you could face

HIPAA violations, as well. The worst of it is that you may not even know that the perpetrators had infiltrated your system until the damage is done and it's too late.

Cyber liability insurance will cover the cost of getting a specialist to come in and figure out how the breach happened and hopefully turn it around. It will even pay for a PR firm. About five years ago, Horizon Blue Cross-Blue Shield of NJ sent out a letter telling their subscribers that employee laptops had been stolen. They didn't even know if their data was breached, but they paid for a year of credit report monitoring for every potentially affected subscriber. Think of all the ancillary costs involved: can you imagine how many of those letters went out? Consider the cost of the offer, the cost of the legal department, the legal firm to help craft that letter, the cost of printing, stuffing the envelopes and mailing them out. Regardless of the amount of coverage for each occurrence, just be aware of the fine print—take note *of the aggregate limit the policy will pay out.* That's the important number.

Let's take another example where this coverage can protect you from costly losses—and the cost of defending lawsuits. Real estate and related bank transactions are vulnerable to phishing scams. In another example, an individual was purchasing a home and received what she believed were the wiring instructions from her attorney. Instead, the funds ended up in a Russian bank. The cybercriminals often intercept emails and put a worm in them. They will mislead you to believe your settlement agent has switched banks.

Cyber insurance will cover these losses, but the carriers want to know that you are taking precautions such as verifying with a known person and having a notarized form signed prior to sending a wire. Otherwise, they may reduce the amount they will pay out.

Special Considerations

While even the best standard insurance policies can't and won't cover everything, special circumstances call for special coverage. There are situations that dictate the need for additional coverages. We will allude to just a few of them. For example, you install an upgraded boiler at your expense for your manufacturing plant, which requires temperature control. Should that boiler explode, your standard liability coverage will not insure the damage and losses to your facility. You need additional coverage for that. Consider the potential damage to property, as well as injuries that would trigger costly lawsuits.

Suppose you are in the process of negotiating a lease for a new facility. During the time when you are fitting up the new facility and transferring all of your equipment and inventory, you leave the old location vacant for 30 days or more. Thieves and vandals break in and steal from you. Bingo! Your insurance carrier does not want to insure you for theft because you left the facility unoccupied.

If you are a third-party service provider such as a moving company, the building landlord will probably expect to see your insurance in the event of possible damage when you are moving a tenant in or out.

If you operate a high-risk business like a night club, you have a higher degree of exposure, due to the risk of fights, for example. This requires coverage for assault and battery. Without it, both the night club operator and the landlord are at risk of getting sued.

Keep in mind that it's not always a clear-cut case of fault. In many situations where loss, damage or injury is involved, there may be contributory negligence. As a result, insurance companies will often settle—or subrogate, which means each party's insurer winds up contributing some portion of the costs. In every case, when it comes to insurance policies, to quote Harvey Topitz, "The big print giveth and the small print taketh away." Even "all risk" coverage doesn't mean every conceivable situation.

Doesn't Everyone Make Mistakes?

Yes. But some mistakes can cost more than others. If you are a professional—a doctor, a lawyer, an accountant, an architect or an engineer—your clients depend on you for accurate representation. Your mistake can cost them big time. Imagine that you are an engineer, and you develop a site plan for the architect who then passes it to the contractor who constructs the building. You neglected to test the soil and it turns out to be contaminated. If you did not have Errors and Omissions Insurance (E&O), you could end up with a major lawsuit.

A large distributor of X-ray equipment and supplies suffered a huge loss when its in-house accountant and bookkeeper embezzled a large sum of money. The auditors failed to catch the activity; the company's payroll bounced, and the business eventually was forced to close. Although the accounting firm had errors and omissions insurance, they were underinsured for the size of the loss.

The Buck Stops Here

Your company grows and you appoint a Board of Directors. Everything seems fine until one of the directors makes a rash, unsupported political statement to the press that does not represent the company's position. In turn, boycotts result and company sales and profits decline. If you had Directors and Officers Insurance (D&O), you might have been able to cover at least some of the losses.

Chapter Five
Failure To Provide A Safe, Secure Work Environment

That's right. It's on you as the owner or executive. A "safe" work environment includes both physical and emotional harm (bullying and verbal harassment) that may come to an employee if the office situation is not properly managed. Realize that workplace safety requirements are a relatively recent concept as far as the law goes, dating back only about 50 years. You can thank labor unions for lobbying to put this legislation in place to protect workers. And while there are specific agencies, such as The Occupational Safety and Health Agency (OSHA), that regulate safety in certain workplaces, all small business owners should be aware of and address a safe work environment for all employees. Government agencies will inspect your business if they believe you have unsafe conditions, not only at the Federal level, but also at the State level—and in some cases, locally. A tenant leasing space in an office may in fact be required to provide fire extinguishers or other equipment to satisfy the local Fire Marshall—or pay a penalty. He or she may even inspect your electrical wiring to be sure it's compliant with local ordinances.

Safety may not only be physical. Employees are protected under federal and state law from harassment and discrimination, whether sexual, racial, religious or otherwise. We delved further into the topic with Andrew Botwin, the principal owner of Strategy, People, Culture – a firm focused on workplace investigations and HR best practices.

At a very high level, harassment and discrimination, in the wake of the "me-too" movement, is a worldwide phenomenon—not just a U.S issue. The truth is harassment, sexual harassment and discrimination protection in the workplace has been around longer than that. At a basic level, the U.S, the Civil Rights Act of 1964 says that employees have the right to go to work free from discrimination—which in turn has over many years included specifically sexual harassment discrimination. Over the years there have been many laws that have been passed, both legislatively and through jurisprudence, that have kind of tacked on a lot of different protected classifications. The federal law says that as an employer, you're automatically liable for the acts of your employees. The U.S. Supreme Court says that's a little harsh in a lot of circumstances, especially when it comes to *intangible* employment actions. Tangible employment actions mean you're fired because you didn't sleep with me.

The Five Commandments of Harassment Law

The *intangible* is a lot of really what happens or allegedly happens in the workplace. For example, I gave the promotion to somebody else. The U.S. Supreme Court said you're still liable as an employer. There's kind of a five-prong test. You lose them if you don't have all five of these things done. The five things are, you need to have policies in place that say we don't allow harassment or discrimination, like written policies. And they need to be distributed and communicated. In addition to having those procedures or those policies, you need to have complaint procedures that say if you've been subjected to this, you're aware of something, you're concerned about something, how to go about making a complaint. In addition to that, you need to have training and the training is supposed to explain what harassment and discrimination is, what to look for, how to identify it and should also cover, at least at a high level, those policies because the courts say, just because you have a policy doesn't mean people understand it. The other two things are that there has to be an investigation. If the organization knew or should have known that there was a potential situation, it has to investigate it objectively. Are you supposed to use an outside investigator? According to the U.S. Supreme Court guidelines, yes. The key is it needs to be looked at in an objective manner. That requires a neutral party. The fifth prong is based on the results of that investigation. The organization needs to take what's called prompt, corrective action. It could be nothing, that could be some type of disciplinary action such as a specialized retraining, or perhaps a warning, or a firing. The standard requires that it be done promptly.

On a federal level, that's one protection mechanism that companies need to implement. Various states and jurisdictions around the country have been passing other laws that either are similar to what the U.S. Supreme court implemented, or their state legislatures may have implemented other laws that mandate something like training. The states can't reduce what's been implemented at the federal level, but they could expand on it. For example, right now in New Jersey, there's not a law that says you have to do training. The New Jersey Supreme Court's case law reiterates the same basic standards we just outlined. New Jersey has one of the deepest histories of being very progressive in terms of employee protections in this space. There's a law called the New Jersey law against discrimination, which predates the Civil Rights Act by close to 20 years. A lot of plaintiffs' attorneys like suing in New Jersey, under state law against discrimination claims as opposed to in federal court, because it's more profitable for them and easier for them to win in those cases. In New Jersey, what's really interesting is they don't have a law mandating the training. but they do have some laws mandating things like settlement agreements and confidentiality/disclosure agreements. In New York, they actually do have a law that mandates training. So, if you're an employer in New York City, for example, pretty much every employer is supposed to by law be doing this. So not only if they don't, they can get sued, they can also get fined. One of Donald Trump's first pieces of legislation included one very small section that actually says that you can no longer deduct attorney fees and settlement costs.

When we refer to sexual discrimination or sexual harassment, if there's unwelcome conduct that's based on a protected class and it meets a certain standard in terms of how far it went--there's largely one universal standard across the country— then you have harassment or discrimination. The rules in terms of how to test for it or interpret it are basically the same. In the seventies, there was the McDonald Douglas Case. In the late nineties there was the Supreme Court rulings in the Ellerth and Faragher cases, which set the federal standards. Essentially, in Ellerth and Faragher, the court ruled that when a supervisor's sexual harassment culminates in a tangible employment action, such as dismissal or an undesirable reassignment, the employer is automatically liable. And in New Jersey, there was a Lehman versus Toys R Us case that kind of set the similar standard in New Jersey. And that predated the U.S. Supreme Court cases too.

If you are an employer, the protected classes that you need to be aware of include, but are not limited to: sex, gender, gender identity, race, religion, creed, national origin, blood trait, disorders, disability, service in the armed forces and veterans. In theory, if an employer has no idea of a person's medical condition, for example, how can they use that as a discriminatory basis? The standard is that the unwelcome conduct has to be based on that protected class. The courts are interpreting some of these things differently today, to some extent, when it comes to age or race, for example.

If you are in a for-profit business, you're in a commercial enterprise, you're making money and you're dealing with the public, it's your obligation to know. You might not know what the speed limit is on the highway. They're going to pull you over if you exceed it. You're going to get a ticket. Not knowing is not a defense with discrimination either.

What about professional service firm partners that are part owners? Are they subject to the same rules requiring harassment training? Recognize that one's gender or position in the company does not exclude them from either harassing or from being harassed by another—whether they are higher or lower on the food chain, so to speak. In 2020, the Supreme Court had a series of rulings where they basically made gender identity a protected class. When we're talking about gender identity, we mean someone who might biologically be a man, let's say, but identifies himself as a female. Prior to that, in over half the states in this country you could have entered into a gay marriage or civil union and then gone into work on Monday and legally been fired because of that reason. That was actually legal discrimination.

Let's address some of the common mistakes that can get an employer sued where discrimination comes into play. For example, dating in the workplace can become a real minefield. Why? Well, one person has to initiate the relationship with the other. If there's a breakup, the person claims that they were harassed, made uncomfortable, forced to engage in the relationship. It's a ticking time bomb. Sometimes people's perspective changes. And sometimes, you know, while some people might not think this is possible, people might agree, but both parties might not really consent. It can also cause disruption in the workplace, depending on how they handle it. When company position becomes involved, such as if you have a subordinate relationship with somebody, it brings into question whether you *can* consent. Because of the pressure, the subordinate may go along with it for fear of losing his or her job. As the employer, what companies need to do to protect themselves or to protect employees can become complicated. You can have a non-fraternization policy and the bigger the business, the odds are somebody is going to date. Then when you discover it, what are you going to do? If you don't enforce the policy consistently, that will leave the company open to employer liability issues.

Then there is the conundrum of multi-state employers with differing requirements. Do they send everyone for training, or just those working in the state that requires it? If you only send the required group, you are leaving yourself open to a challenge from a plaintiff's attorney who will claim that you did not find it important enough to protect his or her client from harassment or discrimination. While you may have Employment Practices Liability Insurance in force, it's becoming more common for the insurance carriers to expect you to have policies and procedures in place in order for them to pay a claim.

Another area of concern involves alcohol. You go out for drinks during happy hour because the company wants to promote camaraderie. What often happens? People say things, they do things, inhibitions are lowered. There are consent issues potentially with drinking as well. Even telling jokes that someone perceives as offensive can result in lawsuits. Employees don't always have the self-awareness they should have. That's where training comes in. The theory behind these states mandating training is just that the better people are trained the less likely to offend someone, or the more sensitive they will be. It's the reason why the courts say if you do all the right things, maybe you can escape liability. Even if you had a bad actor, you've got to take reasonable steps to stop people from making that off color joke.

Sometimes what happens is completely unintentional. In one case, a CEO of a smaller sized insurance company was acquired by a bigger insurance company. They hired a temp. and one day they were alone in the office and he's standing at the door of the copy room, an older guy with the young female. They start talking and mentions what he thinks innocently about how disappointing his marital relationship is. He makes some comments about how pretty she is; he's standing in the doorway, so she feels she's trapped with a creepy old man who's hitting on her. He didn't realize what he was doing. He might have been hitting on her, but not in an evil intentioned way saying he didn't expect anything to happen. but it doesn't matter.

On another note, five people can be standing in a room hearing the same joke. Four can think it's funny as heck. And one could be offended. An example that happened in real life, while I was the head of HR for a company, occurred when Egypt was going through all their unrest. That was at the time where newspapers were more prevalent, and people read headline news. This was what people talked about. Two people in the morning during coffee were talking about this issue, while standing in front of a set of the cubicles. Then one of them realized they had been talking too long, and their way of ending it was saying, "I just think we should blow up the whole Middle East and start all over again." They laughed. It was clearly intended as a lighthearted joke, but there were other people around. Sure enough, somebody sitting in a work station they couldn't see right next to them was Egyptian and had relatives living there. He was actually scared for their safety. The context was not evil intentioned, but he complained, and it became my problem. That demonstrated the lack of sensitivity that people have. People need to learn from it. He didn't file a complaint and it didn't become a legal issue, but it was one that the company had to address. We talk about small employers, how we're very family-like, we don't have to worry about that stuff. That's not true.

Where do you draw the line where you're creating more liability for yourself as an employer, from the person you're firing versus dealing with the issue of the complaint? As a case in point, an executive of a company has a couple related interests that are making him millions and millions of dollars a year. A complaint gets publicized in trade magazines about this person from an employee that worked under his organization 15 to 20 years ago. She never filed a complaint with the company. She's now going public and saying, this person did this to me. In this example, the executive was CEO of a different company now. The company doesn't want the bad press, so they do an investigation and fire this person. He gets counsel to represent him and negotiate whether he's going to leave and under what conditions. The law firm that's counseling him doesn't counsel him on the obligations of an employer to do an investigation. So, they come to a settlement, and he leaves later. The former executive cannot get work. Now he has two law firms, one on the East and one on the West coast representing him in a lawsuit against the law firm that represented him initially. The law firms that are representing him now hired an HR expert to give an expert opinion on what an investigation is because they're claiming that it was a sham investigation. That didn't bode well in favor of the company firing the individual. Public opinion can be much stronger and have quicker momentum than the truth sometimes. Companies have to protect their employees, but also protect their organizations.

As we said before, intent is not the issue. Even if the intent is camaraderie, but it makes someone feel uncomfortable or harassed, it doesn't matter. If they see companies are trying to do the right thing by training their people, they're a lot likelier —even if they're found to be in the wrong, to be more lenient and more reasonable.

Chapter Six
Navigating The Employment Law Minefield

As always, beware the crafty attorney, zealously representing a complaining employee, who points out problems with your company that you never even considered.

For more guidance and information, we consulted with our colleague, Damien Weinstein, of Weinstein+Klein, a New Jersey and New York barred employment law attorney:

To be sure, at the very basic level, in order to stay out of court small business owners should have a handle on employee relations – this includes everything from hiring, promoting, firing, your employee handbook, and compliance with the federal, state, and local laws. We will detail the must-haves for you. In general, just know that the minute you hang out your shingle, you're in business. The minute you hire people, you're in The Twilight Zone. There are numerous things that business owners need to do in order to protect themselves, like having a safe work environment, both physical and emotional. The small business owner also needs to be aware of labor laws, especially when it comes to how to pay your employees.

Another Easy Way for a Small Business Owner to Get Sued
The issue is known as misclassification and it's an easy way to wander into a lawsuit and probably one of the easiest things to screw up. Many small business owners mistakenly believe they can avoid paying payroll taxes and benefits such as workers compensation by paying people on a 1099 when many workers should have been paid on a W-2 instead. W-2 employees have certain rights that independent contractors do not have.

One of the misperceptions involves paying people an amount that may violate a minimum wage, but it doesn't matter because they're an independent contractor. It's become much more prevalent, especially in the modern gig economy. Especially with people working remotely as well, it's not uncommon for multiple employees to be working from home because of COVID. They may have a little side hustle where they're an independent contractor of another company, but because they're not technically an employee, they don't have to report that to their employer, their real employer, their nine to five.

Business owners think, we'll just call you an independent contractor. We'll even put this four-page document that I printed from Google® in front of you that says you are an independent contractor, and you sign it. And so, you're an independent contractor, right? Handshake, great. Everyone moves on until the state comes in and says that doesn't look like an independent contractor to us—or this person turns around and sues you because there's a falling out and he or she says you misclassified them. Remember, the state has an incentive to find this person to be an employee. Audits are conducted by states seeking tax revenue, and it can result in fines in the tens and hundreds of thousands of dollars, depending on how many employees are misclassified. States are ramping up efforts to crack down on misclassification, and that means both increased enforcement and heftier penalties.

The IRS has a very specific legal test to qualify as an independent contractor. First and foremost, if they only work for you, they are almost assuredly an employee. Think about what this person is doing. What level of control do you have over that person, what company resources is that person using, does that person provide similar services to other companies at the same time? Those answers are really what's going to suggest to you whether this person is an employee or not. Here's a red flag: you can't have two people serving the same function for the same company but are paid and treated differently. One has benefits. One doesn't; one has protections under the laws against discrimination. While companies struggle with their profit margins going down, they are willing to roll the dice and see what happens—until they're negotiating a quarter million dollar fine. States are really cracking down on this.

New Jersey Division of Labor uses an "ABC" Test. Per New Jersey Unemployment Compensation Law, a worker should be considered an employee unless all the following circumstances apply: (1) The individual has been and will continue to be free from control or direction over the performance of work performed, both under contract of service and in fact; and (2) the work is either outside the usual course of the business for which such service is performed, or the work is performed outside of all the places of business of the enterprise for which such service is performed; and (3) the individual is customarily engaged in an independently established trade, occupation, profession or business. If you don't meet all three prongs of the test, you're an employee. No ifs, ands or buts.

For example, let's say you hire a virtual assistant, and that person has a legitimate business. You contract with them for a certain number of hours. They're working with a lot of customers, and they could fire you at any time and you could fire them, and they do the work around their schedule. But if you have your own assistant and she just happens to work virtually that doesn't make her a 1099 independent contractor.

The assumption is independent contractors have no rights. Employees have all the rights and that's part of the problem. The state wants people to have rights in the workplace, but the state also wants to be able to tax people and extract their pound of flesh from the employment model. In certain jurisdictions, New York and California, they have extended protections for independent contractors because they know so much of the economy is this gig economy where you've got these independent contractors. New York State, and also New York City are extending really stringent anti-harassment, anti-sexual discrimination policies in the workplace. They need to have mandatory training for all your employees every single year. You must have a certificate that they attended. You have to maintain those certificates of attendance for six years. And now that also applies to their 1099 pool. Classification of employees versus independent contractors varies by industry. It's so complicated and the guidance is changing constantly—particularly when there is a shift in the controlling political party with a differing philosophy.

How serious can this get? It may depend on where your business is located. New Jersey is cracking down really hard. There is potential criminal and jail time for repeated violations of this. That's somewhat of a newer development. The double whammy is that you treated this person like an independent contractor, but he or she is actually an employee so now you have to pay all those back taxes, payroll taxes, workers comp retroactively, possibly overtime pay at time and a half—and that's where the state will audit and find a penalty. That could break a small business. The numbers really are extraordinary when it comes to employer's liability and ways that companies are getting sued. That's why it really is important to get an attorney upfront, preferably an employment attorney who can guide you on these matters.

Protect Yourself Early in the Hiring Process

So, how soon do you need to get counsel involved? Well, believe it or not, your legal liability as an employer (or an "about to be" employer) starts with the second you put out a job posting or description of your job. People gloss over the onboarding process. There are a lot of ways you can screw up putting out a job description and it could be seemingly innocent. For example, there could be references to gender. There could be references to certain, continuous employment. If you put an ad up for a job and it's racially discriminatory in the way it's written, somebody else who's looking for a job could actually file a complaint with the Department of Labor or sue you. The state could always crack down, but what's going to happen is invariably someone will apply. They will not get a job offer, or they might not even get an interview. And they'll say that it was because it was based on some form of discrimination. Employment law is essentially common sense. You've got issues where it's like, men preferred, like must have continuous, no criminal history or non-smokers only. Putting things out like that are red flags. As an attorney, we call it "disparate impact." If you put certain restrictions on employee applications in your job description, you're basically signaling to certain demographics or certain classes who might be disproportionately impacted by that, that they need not apply. Even if you find that you win your day in court, who wants to go to court?

Times have changed. How many businesses get sued because they asked the young female applicants if they're married, if they're dating, if they plan on having kids, or when they plan on having kids? It was acceptable in 1945, but not today. The interview process is full of traps. States are legalizing marijuana; there's the whole issue with pre-screening employees. That's an interesting, evolving area of the law. Even if marijuana is legal, obviously you don't want them to smoke marijuana on the job. That's an intoxication issue. Consider that in theory, you could test positive for marijuana in your system and not have smoked that day or that week. That's part of the problem; you might have people who are under the influence, or it's in their system. The issue is whether they are actually impaired and if it would impact their performance.

Once you get past advertising the job and the interviewing process, and you have actually made the decision to bring somebody on, that's really where employment lawyers get to shine because an attorney puts together your employment offer, the I-9 verification, which is required to make sure that this person is authorized to work in the country, conditioning their offer of employment on that. Even if you know that the person's an American citizen, you still have to do it. Technically you're supposed to do it no later than three days before their first day of employment, or their start date. You're supposed to have everything filled out; it could be an offer letter. It could be an employment agreement. Employees are still "at will" for the most part. You're going to always want to put that in their offer letter. Anything that you put in front of them, an offer letter, an NDA, absolutely a handbook—put in there that they are an at-will employee, which means that they could be fired, or they could leave for any reason or no reason whatsoever, so long as it's not an unlawful reason.

What does that come down to? Well, crazy as it may sound, if Bob walks into your office one day wearing a blue shirt and you just hate the color blue, you can fire him. There's nothing illegal about that. That's not a protected class—people with blue shirts. Conversely, if you fired him because you don't like the color of his skin, or fire her because she's pregnant or because he's gay, you are exposed to a discrimination lawsuit. Your offer letter is basically going to have your rate of pay, your start date, your at will status, whether you're exempt or non-exempt, (exempt employees are exempt from overtime. They are deemed by law to not be entitled to time and a half pay—usually higher-level executives) and whom you report to. It's also important to have choice of law. We'll define that next.

If you're going to have an arbitration provision, put that front and center, bold, in all caps. Make sure it's clear because courts really do not like to enforce arbitration provisions against employees unless it was really obvious, so just make sure it wasn't buried in the contract somewhere. Arbitration keeps things out of court. It is usually a quicker resolution and the idea of keeping it out of court is, more so because of the bad PR, the public record. It may be a bit more expensive because you've got arbitration fees. The cost of arbitration acts as a deterrent to employees who might otherwise sue because the employee has to pay his or her share of the arbitration costs. Sometimes it helps with pre-suit or pre arbitration negotiations by providing some leverage because you, as the company, can say, "Listen, if you really feel strongly about this potential claim, go file an arbitration". Then you've got the employee who might be a minimum wage worker or who might be a secretary. It might be somebody who isn't sitting on a hefty pile of cash. They have to make the determination of whether it's worth investing the cash just for the arbitration fee alone, let alone the attorney's fees. You could also go to non-binding mediation first and if that doesn't work out, then go to arbitration. In that case, put that in the agreement as well as in your offer letter.

Your Best Defense: Put Your Policies in Writing

The next main document in terms of onboarding is going to be the handbook, too often overlooked by small business owners. This is not a heavy lift for companies. It's not as expensive as they probably think, but it is much more important than they think it is. You have to set the rules up as an employer. What days do you get off? What do you or don't you get paid for? What benefits are available? When do you qualify for them? There are legal requirements like Paid Time Off and sick leave now. Unfortunately, the first misconception is that handbooks are optional. This depends on the jurisdiction, but in some places the law says you have to have a handbook. At the very least, there are laws that say this policy needs to be given in writing. Writing it in a handbook qualifies to satisfy the law. But wait—there's more! The handbook is super important because you've got these required disclosures and notices that you have to provide to your employees. You now have to provide notices about certain COVID protections and COVID measures and paid leave under FCRA in writing. It's a convenient way to consolidate all of these important documents in one place and get them into your employees' hands. It should be updated annually. If it's something like a COVID addendum or rider, you can literally just issue that as a standalone. You always want your employees to sign and acknowledge receiving it.

In addition to your EEO statement, which states that you don't discriminate in employment opportunities, is your anti- harassment statement and perhaps most importantly, your complaint procedure. How are employees able to report violations and to whom do they report it? What will the company do? In investigating, will the employee who reports it be expected to cooperate with that investigation, will it be kept confidential to the best of the company's ability? Is there also an anti-retaliation provision? It's always a good idea to let your employees know what their rights and obligations are as an employee in the workplace.

In keeping with the purpose of this book, just know that if an employer is getting sued for retaliation, or for permitting sexual harassment in the workplace, one of the first things the plaintiff's attorney is going to ask for in discovery is a copy of the handbook. At least your policy is in it. If you don't have it, they're going to say, "Your honor, this company does not take this seriously. They couldn't even put together a simple two-page policy on preventing harassment in the workplace." The attorney's also going to want proof that his client got the handbook and signed off acknowledging he or she read it and that they understand it. Also, it's in that person's primary language. You want to maintain those records. And if you have the technology for it, set up some sort of portal where you can have this constantly accessible, so an employee can simply log on and look at it instead of going to HR or the business owner. If there's no HR, it's a smaller company, they can just pop on and read the policy. It also serves almost like a frequently asked questions type of document.

How do you go about putting together a handbook that will stand up to scrutiny if it's challenged in a lawsuit? Several of the payroll companies provide these services to smaller employers. There's a misconception that lawyers will come in and just tear them up. Not true. These things are usually 80 to 90% good. The problem is they're not specific to different companies. They're kind of uniform. There might be things that don't apply based on the number of employees the company has, for example. That's going to create some confusion. In the case of a PEO, where you lease your employees, typically you're going to have some sort of joint employer rule when it comes to who is liable. In that case, it depends on the nuances and who controls the hours and the job duties, etc.

In the interest of keeping this contemporary, there are considerations relating to each different jurisdiction that can affect your policies in the handbook. For example, because of COVID, businesses have employees working in different States. Perhaps you live in New Jersey, but your company is headquartered in New York. Now you're working full-time from home in New Jersey. Perhaps because of COVID you went to a different state. It can't be because you went to your mom's house in Maine and you're working from Maine. That doesn't make you subject to the Maine rules. So, what determines which rules apply? There is a dependence on how long you were there and whether it has become your program's presence. If you've got employees now in different States, which a lot of companies do, you have to be mindful that you might be subject to those States' employment laws. If that's the case, then you need to have a specific identity in your handbook that addresses those specific rules. Handbooks may have to be customized to the various states where your employees are working because you've got employees there and you're subject to those rules and requirements.

Document, Document, Document Employee Under Performance

The task at hand for the employer involves documenting if they're underperforming, they're coming in late or logging on late, there are performance issues or something that you need to correct. You must provide written warnings and notifications to employees that they are not performing up to par, which requires having some sort of written log and evidence. If and when you fire that person, they may go to a lawyer and they may say that they were fired because they're over 60, they're a woman, they're black, Hispanic, white, or perhaps they're homosexual. If that obviously applies, the first thing you need to be able to show is that this person was fired for bad performance. Not because he's homosexual, black, etc.

We get the attorney demand letter saying we think this person was fired because of these protected characteristics. The first thing you do is say to the client, give me your written records, showing that this person was a poor performer, because I'm going to share that with the other side.

I want them to know you've got a claim. Here's a page of documentation or 15 electronic files that show this person was a bad apple from the day they started. Do you really want to litigate this case right now in that scenario? It still might be worth paying a little something for that person to go away, but that's obviously a business decision. As we discuss in another chapter, Employment Liability Insurance is definitely a good thing to have, especially once you start getting above a certain number of employees.

In today's world, with such a highly regulated business environment, there are numerous requirements to provide notifications like the posters you typically see in the break room. They exist at the federal, state and depending on the jurisdiction, like New York City, even at the local level. Certain things have to be communicated to employees. For example, often half in English, half in Spanish, about worker safety or over time and minimum wage. It's an interesting issue now that a lot of people are virtual, as to how those things get disseminated. No one's gathering around the coffee maker anymore in the office. You probably need to disseminate that via email or some sort of community portal that everyone can access. Like the handbook, notices are important because they're legally required, but it also shows that you take the law seriously. It's an easy fix. These simple practices set the tone for the right employer-employee relationship.

"Every interaction you have with your employees as an employer is a potential liability."

Consider that every interaction you have with your employees as an employer is a potential liability. You can never eliminate it entirely, but you can minimize it. There are probably three States that are the worst states to be an employer based on the legal requirements that are on you and the legal benefits that are available to your employees. They are New Jersey, New York and California. An employee can screw up and you can fire that employee. But if you mess up one little thing, you might have a federal issue. The perfect example is COVID. We are advising all of our clients that they need to have a written COVID policy, what the company is doing to keep employees safe, who they can report concerns to, what the response will be. It follows CDC and OSHA guidelines, maybe state guidelines too. If somebody gets sick, you can demonstrate that we've got this great policy, we've invested time, energy, and money into these resources to put together a COVID protocol. Part of it is to be able to say to the plaintiff's attorney, or to be able to say to the court or the arbitrator, we take this very seriously. Here's an example of how seriously we take it. We've got attorneys, we've got policies, we've got disclosures, we've got signed acknowledgement forms. Perhaps we have employee trainings on certain things. It's part optics, it's part legal defense and the two go hand in hand.

Safety First!

OSHA, the Occupational Safety and Health Administration, has a standard. The idea is that you should be safe from *reasonably known* hazards. What constitutes a reasonably known hazard? It depends on the industry. It depends on the workplace. COVID, for example, is a reasonably known hazard. Companies have an obligation to try to do everything they can to keep COVID out of the workplace. This is why you should have written policies in place. Known hazards could be heavy machinery or even syringes. You have to take steps to minimize the risk of some sort of mishap. You need to notify employees of those hazards and at least educate them to make sure that this is as safe of a work environment as you can provide. Ultimately, it applies to everyone. Obviously, the level of risk and how seriously you have to take it and what measures you have to put in place depends upon your type of business.

The hot question right now revolves around people returning to the workplace post-COVID. As a general matter, you can require employees to come back. There's no right to stay home. There might be exemptions that are based on underlying medical conditions, which can be documented, which sounds like a request for an accommodation. On the other hand, anxiety alone about returning to the workplace is not enough to get you an accommodation. Concurrent with that, can the employer require the employee to get vaccinated against COVID? Theoretically yes you can. There are two exemptions, medical conditions and sincerely held religious beliefs. However, you don't want to be asking them about their medical conditions. It's a bad path to travel down. Don't do it. The better thing to do would be to put out feelers for people on their vaccination status. If an employee says, yes, I am vaccinated, you generally can ask that employee to show proof with a vaccination card. If the employee says, no, I am not vaccinated, stop there. Don't ask why, because you might get the religious reason. You might get the medical reason in New Jersey. There's a specific exemption for pregnant women. Why is that a problem? You might get a young woman who says, "Oh, I didn't get vaccinated and I'm not getting vaccinated because of my pregnancy" and the employer is saying, I don't need to know this. Perhaps four months down the road, you want to fire that employee for perfectly legitimate reasons. She can now say you forced me to disclose to you that I was pregnant. I think you fired me because you knew I was pregnant. You probably knew I was going to request maternity leave.

One further thought on regulatory requirements that can turn into lawsuits. Disability is now considered a protected class in alleged cases of discrimination. The ADA, Americans With Disabilities Act, requires an employer to provide reasonable accommodation for employees with handicaps—and not to discriminate against them in hiring, promotion or firing. Reasonable accommodation can mean anything from having ramps along with stairs to enter the workplace, to elevators, to signs in Braille. Spoiler alert: even your website must now be considered ADA compliant and accessible to those with adaptive or assistive devices. Yes, suits are being filed over this as we speak. For the basics, visit: webaccessibility.com.

Chapter Seven
Neglecting Debts And Not Paying Bills And Obligations In A Timely Manner

What better way to invite a lawsuit than not fulfilling your obligations? Businesses run on cash flow and rarely can operate without some sort of financing or outside capital. When you are "bootstrapping" your company, especially in its early days, staying current with payments, maintaining good credit (or building a credit history for the business) will be essential to obtaining and maintaining access to this capital, whether through some sort of borrowing or by raising outside capital investment. Don't kid yourself. As a startup, unless you already have outside funding, your personal credit is absolutely essential to securing that first line of business credit. Know this—as much as you would like to avoid it, you may have to personally guarantee that first loan, as well. A skilled accountant or lending professional (look for an independent consultant) can help with financial documentation that will paint a picture of your stability and ability to pay.

According to Marco Carbajo in a December 5th, 2019 blog article on the SBA website, if you operate as a sole proprietorship, it's important to understand there is no legal or financial separation between you and your business. If that's the case, when you obtain credit or apply for funding, all activity will be solely tied to you as an individual and reflected on your personal credit reports.

To keep your business and personal finances separate, the first step is to start building credit in your company's name. If you want to build business credit quickly here are five simple steps.

Step 1 – To make your business a distinct legal entity requires that you select a business structure such as an LLC, LLP or corporation. Remember, sole proprietorships do not create a separate business entity. Once you form your business entity, the next step is to register your business. This particular step is dependent on your structure and where your business is located.

For additional support on choosing the right structure for your company and registration be sure to check out the SBA's Business Guide.

Step 2 – You should apply for a federal tax ID for your company. You can obtain it for free using the IRS assistance tool (be wary of "pay for" services). This is a nine-digit number assigned to your company which you will use for things such as filing company tax returns, opening a business bank account, applying for licenses and permits, and applying for business credit.

Step 3 – Once you have your federal tax ID, you'll want to open a business bank account for your company. This is a mandatory step in creating a clear separation between your business and personal expenses. Your banking relationships play an important role in your company's funding potential. Not only does your business bank account serve as a bank reference on credit applications, it also provides key data that lenders use during a funding review.

Step 4 – One of the easiest ways to build business credit is to apply for net terms with vendors and suppliers. As you buy supplies, inventory, or other materials on credit, those purchases and payments get reported to business credit reporting agencies. This activity creates your company's credit profile and business credit report. After your company has several trade lines reporting, a business credit rating (score) is generated. Remember, it's important to select vendors and suppliers that report to a business credit reporting agency. Each relationship you have also serves as a trade reference that can be used on future credit applications as well.

Step 5 – There are three major business credit reporting agencies so it's important to monitor each of your company credit files. Each agency collects data from various sources and may have different information about your company.

The good news is each of the business credit agencies provide a way for you to update basic information about your business. If you uncover any outdated or incorrect information, you'll want to contact the agency to make the appropriate change.

With an established business credit report, you may get higher credit approvals, better interest rates and repayment terms on loans and lines of credit.

It's equally important to establish a diversity of accounts with other types of business credit such as a business credit card or line of credit. Let these five simple steps serve as a starting point to building business credit for your company.

If you are served with a lawsuit for the collection of a business debt, Attorney Steven Mitnick advises, initially you probably want to get an attorney to file answers. Sooner or later, you're going to get judgments against you, but you probably could buy six months to a year by just filing an answer. The attorney will hash out the details and buy you time while you decide if you're going to be a candidate for a liquidation or a reorganization. It gives you some breathing space to make a decision whether you want to file a bankruptcy or a state court insolvency or you just want to shut down. Just be aware that the Fair Debt Collection Practices Act does not apply to commercial debt. You should also know that the plaintiff does not have to give you a notice. They can just file suit.

You may have a situation where people are thinking they're walking away from their debt because they're liquidating their company or filing for bankruptcy, and it could be fraudulently transferred to a third party—possibly a secured creditor. The proper way involves an assignment for the benefit of creditors, which avoids bankruptcy and assures that all creditors' debts will be considered in the event of a corporation liquidation.

If you allegedly owe money, somebody's going to have to move for summary judgment and there's always a factual issue that can be raised. Here is the important point: *they have to prove that you owe the money. The burden is on the plaintiff.* Perhaps you never received the product. That creates a factual issue which delays the case and has to get hashed out in discovery or trial. If your attorney is on defense, he or she will put in an answer and dig into the facts, which takes time. There's a lot of accounting going through records and figuring—and there's a lot of difference of opinion.

Let's look at the issue from the other side. If you are the business owner and you're owed money, what kind of steps do you need to take besides just filing suit in order to protect yourself? The reality is that by the time you find out that you are not going to be paid, it's probably too late. If you do it in the beginning, you could always take a lien on the defendant's assets to secure yourself, but most creditors don't do that. (Like a UCC filing.) However, there needs to be an affirmative agreement to do that. Consider that the assets may already be encumbered by other creditors. You should run a lien search to see how many people are in front of you, but it's taken too long already. Another option is to take a personal guarantee.

First and foremost, as we have said throughout this book, put things in writing ahead of time. For example, you can't get attorney's fees and collection costs if you don't have it written down and agreed to in advance. While every case is facts sensitive, if they sign, they are probably obligated to it.

Who is liable for the debts—you or your company? If the principals are named defendants based upon fraud or misrepresentation, they may be held liable for the corporation's debts. Let's say your company owes money and the creditor sues you personally, too. Then you have to file an answer denying liability. Always check the lawsuits that come in and make sure you're not named personally. Even if the company went bankrupt it could come back to haunt you later. You have to make a motion to vacate the judgment and there's certain grounds for that. Some are only available for the first year and some are always available. Pay attention when you get served with things. If they name you personally, you need to deal with that now, not 10 years from now when you're selling your house. If they served the company and not you, you may have the defense of bad service. If you're involved in companies and those companies go out of business, you should always do searches and protect yourself. If you have a small company and there's a handful of employees, you should let your staff know that if any Constable or court officer comes in with a lawsuit, you're the only one that can accept it.

While accustomed to looking at it through the creditor's standpoint, we are now viewing the subject from the debtor's perspective, which is much different. So, how can a debtor make it a lot easier? In Jonathan Bender's words, if you want to understand defense, you need to understand offense. We asked Mr. Bender, in private practice handling commercial collections for 25 years, what legitimate things you can do, and what he sees that debtors do wrong when their creditors are looking to get paid.

Let's look at an example. If you're going to a commercial bank and they're issuing a large commercial loan, more likely than not, there's going to be collateral involved. But there is a big industry of alternative lenders that businesses go to, and they pay high interest rates. Maybe they can't get a conventional business loan, so they go to these alternative lenders. These tend to be very, very high interest rates and, not collateralized. These alternative lenders also include cash advances. In a typical scenario, a cash advance, as opposed to an actual loan to a retailer, a dry cleaner, or a liquor store that needs a hundred thousand dollars, will have to sell them future receivables of maybe $130,000 over the course of, let's say a year. If that were a loan, it would be a 30% interest rate. But it's not. Sometimes it's even over a shorter period of time than a year. $130,000 over six months is actually 60%.

Now, let's examine a more customary situation from the creditor's side first. For nearly every business, selling on credit is a virtual necessity. Unless your customers are willing and able to pay upfront, the business needs to extend credit. The advice to every business is simply to have advantageous sales terms. You can find sales terms either in a credit application or you can include them conspicuously on your invoices. Or, if you have just a general contract with your customer, include them in the contract. When is it more enforceable and when is it less enforceable, on an invoice versus on a contract?

From basic contract law, once you've established a course of business where you've put your customer on notice that these are the terms, then silence would be considered acquiescence. What are the key terms that the creditor should have? It's important to incentivize your customer to pay you. Suing your customer should be a last resort, so how do you motivate them? If your customer's still in business, the lights are on and the phones are ringing, then they're paying somebody. The key is to prioritize the creditor. If the customer can't pay everyone due to their circumstances, you can make it expensive for him not to pay you. Make them pay you interest if they pay late, and (reasonable) attorney fees if you have to sue them. Put that in your sales terms. Typically, what's common is one and a half percent monthly interest, which to 18%. Even if a particular state has rules that apply to commercial transactions, they are not going to totally negate the provision; they might modify it. In that case, a judge isn't going to strike the contract, but instead will modify your terms to conform to the law. As to what would be considered reasonable attorney's fees, often 30 to 33% of the outstanding balance will be deemed reasonable. That said, The American model for legal fees is that each side pays its own lawyer unless there's a specific basis for shifting the fee. A basis for shifting fees would be either a court rule, a statute or a contract. So, barring any court rule, if you don't have it in writing, you have to pay your own lawyer.

What information from a creditor's standpoint should be included on a credit application? First, the exact legal name of the customer, their tax ID number, so you can do searches for any judgments, and to do a bank search. With small business owners, consider requesting social security numbers of the principals— generally if you are requiring a personal guarantee. In some cases, you might not even be able to get a credit report on a small or newly established business. As always, lawyers can give advice, but business owners need to be flexible. The terms should be prominently displayed on your credit application or your contract; if they are "buried", that might invalidate the agreement.

"Don't hide from your creditors."

Now, let's look at it from the debtor's side of the table. They often make mistakes such as poor negotiation, not willing to keep up their end of the bargains, transferring assets away, fraudulent conveyances.

These and other errors can get them in trouble. Your best advice, according to attorney Jon Bender: don't hide from your creditors. If the issue is your ability to pay, get ahead of the issue. Contact your supplier and let them know that you're not hiding from it, that you are having a problem. Ask them to work with you. If I'm your supplier, I don't want to have to sue you for a number of reasons. For one, suing you is expensive for me. It's not easy to sue; it's not easy to collect on a judgment. It's not cheap. You have to pay a lawyer and they can drag out a lawsuit. From a creditor's standpoint, I'd rather work with you and preserve the relationship. Put simply, if you go legal on your customer, then you've burned that bridge. You will never do business with this person again. From the customer's perspective, contact your supplier and say that you want to make good on the debt. Ask if they can work something out; ask for payment terms.

There are always options. For example, if you go to arbitration, while there are advantages to it, you are giving up your day in court. You can get an arbitrary ruling and that arbitrary ruling might not be appealable. Mediation is a good thing. It could be formal, or it could be informal. Once you are in a lawsuit, your lawyers owe it to their clients to try to work together. The hostility should never be between the lawyers. In the end there's almost always a deal because we recognize that the lawyers should be brokering the deals for the clients.

Chapter Eight
Failure To Create A "Well-Thought Out" Business Plan

Failing to create a "well-thought out" plan is somewhat of a generous statement. More often than not, I find businesses that do not have a written plan of any kind. They may have information about their products or services, but they rarely have a plan or working document that addresses operations, marketing, sales, financials, etc. I have yet to find a business that succeeds without a written business plan. It does not have to be an "MBA grade" document with graphs, charts and significant analysis. It just needs to be a writing that helps you explore and address all the strengths, weaknesses, opportunities and threats (SWOT) of the business and industry. It should also help you work out the costs (both product related and operational) and profitability of the business. Is your product or service priced not only in keeping with the marketplace, but also high enough to create a significant profit to make your efforts worthwhile? By the way, if these two (market price and price needed for profitability) do not line up, you should rethink your business (or at least the product). There are very skilled business consultants, business lawyers, outside CFOs, etc… that can help guide and work with you on your business plan. And even if you have been in operation for some time, it is never too late to get to work on a plan of your own. Business plans should be living documents that you review periodically and update as needed. Business conditions change. Industries change. Customers and products change. Times change. You may need to change with them. Your business plan should reflect those changes as they occur.

Jay Allen, in his book *#ADDAZERO, The Ultimate Guide to Significant and Sustainable Scale – Establishing Base Camp*, identified 3 common flaws that led to businesses and even industries' failure in various sectors across the UK. One of the three flaws identified was the failure of the business to have a written business plan. "I have met multiple business owners, some of them quite sizeable businesses, who would argue, *'I've got this far without one; why do I need to start now?'* And the simple fact is: Unless you have a business plan, you are still driving blind!" Your plan must be in writing, so you can share it with others and receive the benefit of their input and insight. "[T]he problem with a plan that's 'in your head' is that it is in YOUR head. Without documenting it and sharing it with others, only you will have the slightest idea as to whether you are heading in the right direction or not." Mr. Allen also points out that your business plan, even if written, must be a "living" document, kept up to date and kept at the front of mind as all critical business decisions are made.

We consulted Joann Seery in South Carolina, an expert in creating and advising business owners on effective business planning. Why do business owners really need a business plan? First, it's a roadmap, a guide that really will take you step by step through the process of your business or through the growth of your business. Often, business owners are so excited that everybody's going to use their product or services and life is going be great. Then they quickly get frustrated because their expectations don't match up with reality. A well formulated business plan takes everything they have in their head, puts it through step by step and assigns triggers and financials, assigning numbers to things. This helps the business owner to plan and to achieve measurable results. The business plan helps to put a clearer perspective of what the business owner can expect from their business. Most important, it helps the owner to know if they are really making money.

Consider this real-world business story. A very small food manufacturing company received a huge order on a regular basis through Macy's. However, by not planning properly, they ended up losing money because they didn't price the product correctly. They didn't have the staff to produce the product and the situation actually ended up closing them down. If you haven't thought it through and you haven't determined exactly what the cost is for each and every bottle of jam or every client you get, it will become a recipe for disaster. Even the business plan writer needs to have a solid business plan for his or her own business.

If you are either very talented or really want to put in a lot of time, you can write your own business plan—but at some point, you need help and guidance along the way. While there are probably eight to ten sections of a really well written business plan, there are four major ones if we boiled it down to categories to start with. So, where do you start and where do you go from there?

The first thing that's really important is to understand what your mission or vision is for your company. You have to have a clear understanding of exactly why you are going into business and go through an introspective process that really determines your emotional and intellectual reasons behind starting this business. It will also help you go through the highs and lows of your business because no matter how long you've been in business or how well you do business, you will have those days. Second, mission and vision help you determine your target market and your pricing. You need to articulate why you're doing the business, who you're going do it with from a sales standpoint, who's going to help you and what is your personality? There's your product, there are your people, there's your marketing and then there's the numbers—your financials. Those are the four major categories. Beyond that is the issue of how are you going to do it? Very important—you're never going to pay yourself unless you do it from the very beginning. A major corollary to that: if you don't start out paying your taxes on time, you'll always be behind.

When you examine the numbers, it begs the question of whether the business is viable or are you just working? Right. If you can't pay yourself, if you're just barely paying your bills, then you can't even sell it to anybody either.

"You Can't Do It All On Your Own."

Another area that is really important is having a team of trusted advisors. You may not necessarily be paying them, but you always have someone that is like a mentor—someone who has been in your industry longer than you have. You can ask them what are the challenges that they had to overcome? What are some of the insights that you need to know? When you first start out, one of the things you can do every month, try to have a cup of coffee with someone that you were referred to—not to do business directly, but to ask them questions about why they were successful or the problems that they had and how they overcame them instead of just spending the next 20 years, trying to figure it out on your own. Even meet with your banker or the SCORE or your local SBA office. Use those people as resources and mentors to help you through your business. You can create your own advisory board, even if you have a small company, with just one or two people. You help them; they help you. You meet once a quarter and you just share ideas. You can't do it on your own.

Beyond your initial business plan, it's also important to have strategic plans because you can get in a lot of trouble spending money, have it totally ineffective and not reach anybody, not reach the right people or not even resonate with anybody. Keep in mind that the most important part of having a business plan is reviewing it on a regular basis. It's a living, breathing document that you need to use—not put on a shelf and forget about. It can grow and change and modify. Maybe you don't even end up in the same kind of business you thought you were going into because it wasn't viable, or you didn't like it as much. That's okay. You just still need a roadmap to get there.

You need to monitor what is working and what isn't working—especially for your PR or for your sales forecast. Then you have to go back and figure out why you didn't sell as many items as you thought you would and make adjustments so everything will work the way it should. Then you can meet the demand and you're not overspending and you're following that budget you set. When that's done, figure out why, but don't spend any more, especially with marketing.

Let's examine the financials because if you're a little skilled with a spreadsheet, you can list your revenue and the different products you might sell. Then you can come up with a list of expenses. You do need to do projections but know that they will change so don't do them too far out. If you're going to present the business plan to somebody who's lending you money or going to invest in your business, you certainly want the financials to look good.

First of all, you need to have a good amount of money to get your business going. People often underestimate it. Working capital is going to be imperative as far as how long you stay in business. Understand that just because you open the doors doesn't mean you're going to get customers right away. Have enough working capital, like savings to float you for at least a year. Even if your business is five or six months from opening, start networking, start marketing now and keep the marketing budget to a minimum. Show them pictures of what you do and ask if they have any connections that they can help you with. Look up industry trends. There's so much information that you can get from your local county government website, see sales in certain areas, then research how many shops there are and get a feeling of what the spending is in the area. Join associations and professional organizations that are particular to your industry and make informed decisions. Then make your projections that way. Always project low because you would rather be pleasantly surprised.

When putting together the financials, do month to month. Use a basic Excel spreadsheet, listing what you budgeted for sales, your projections and your expenses. This is your net—your profit or a loss. Then have a blank column right next to it and every month go back and fill that in with the actuals. Then you'll start seeing trends and you'll see where you can make adjustments. For example, if you think that you're going to do so much revenue and you're not, then you're going to have to bring down the expenses. Ask what are the variable costs that you can control? What are the fixed costs that you're not going to be able to control? Keep your overhead low and once the business starts coming in, then you can look at other options. Don't sign a 10-year lease thinking you're just going to make the money and make it up because you're going to get in trouble.

Even if you're writing your business plan yourself, have somebody else review it and give it a reality check. Professional business plan writers might not know your industry but their ability to research may prove that your numbers don't make sense. Again, do the research and speak to people in the industry. They're the ones that have made the mistakes and made the adjustments.

One business owner after only four months had to close his doors. He admitted that he didn't write a business plan. He needed to get out of a 10-year lease for the space, as well as figure out what to do with $3,000 of equipment that he had leased. It was just a mess. Like so many, he was so excited developing the recipes and looking at the machine that made the food and developing the whole concept, what the restaurant would look like, but failed to determine where was he getting the customers? He couldn't even explain why he was charging his prices.

Let's look at other pitfalls or traps people fall into when they fail to do a proper plan. As in the story above, a big one is that they just really don't have any plan. Another one for many involves determining the correct location. Who are your customers? Once again, without a written plan and the research, you can't make a good, informed decision. Doing a competitive analysis is great because you see what other people are doing and you see trends, what is working because they're all doing it.

Understanding what you want to get out of the business is important. What exit strategy do you want? That can change as well as anything else, but are you starting this business because you want to sell it someday? Do you want to pass it on to a family member? Do you want to have an employee take it over? It really makes a difference on how you operate the business and grow the business in the future. You have to see what are they buying? You built a name. Do you have a loyal staff? Maybe there are no operational systems to run the business where somebody can take it over.

Conversely, you might think you're going to keep the business until you're 70 or 80 years old but then someone comes to you and makes you an offer for the business. Have someone that you can reach out to and say, is this a good deal? Should I do it now?

That's why business failure rates are so high—because of all this lack of planning. That's the theme of this book, to a large extent a lot of it is about planning, putting things in writing, having a business agreement with your partner and dealing with customers in writing.

As we have discussed, in addition to your business plan you need clear, written agreements. A lot of the creative people like photographers and musicians—their work is out there, and people are using it and they're not supposed to. They have a contract that says, this does not transfer to you, and you don't have the right to use it until you pay the bill. They can only use it for this limited purpose.

If you're in business, you have to act like you're serious about this. Serious, responsible business people have business plans, and those business plans become operational manuals. They have an employee handbook, they have their financials, they have their marketing guide and their product manual. They have consistent branding. It's all part of what started as a business plan and became a working document or a volume of documents because they used it and it evolved over time. It doesn't have to be a hundred pages at first, but you need to have the basics. Do it in phases. For example, phase one is just yourself. Then when you reach say $10,000 a month in revenue, it's going to be you and a part time person; that's phase two. When you hit this financial trigger or this sales trigger, then you'll move on to the next phase, so it definitely grows over time. Being aware that you're going to need to add those things onto your plan is very important. Having milestones like that and benchmarks are street signs along the road and are important.

You can even do what they call the lean canvas—it's a one-page thing with boxes to start thinking about things that become a written plan. Just start with a vision board. While your vision's not going to make any money that's part of the business plan exercise, it will help figuring out whether your idea works.

While not having a business plan in and of itself won't get you sued, many of the mistakes you may make by not having thought through and planned for important business issues could in fact put you on the wrong side of a suit. If you are starting out and bootstrapping your business, you can find guidance on creating a business plan from the US Small Business Administration or from your local SCORE counselor. For those of you who are still "old school," you might even find a CD languishing on the shelves of an office supplies store with business plan software. But more commonly today, plans can be created using online resources. Nerdwallet.com lists the top five business plan software platforms on their blog for January 7, 2021. They are as follows*:

•LivePlan: affordable, pay-as-you go, template rich online platform.
•GoSmallBiz: touted as best for managing multiple businesses.
•Enloop: simple and fast with a 7-day free trial.
•BizPlan: best for startups looking for funding or investors.
•PlanGuru: best for financial planning and budgeting.

*As time passes, options change. Be sure to do your own research when choosing the best platform for your business.

Chapter Nine
Failing To Follow Appropriate And
Formal Business Procedures

Business organizations, such as LLCs, corporations or partnerships, allow multiple persons to do business together creating products and services for sale. But they also create a level of protection against personal liability of the underlying owners (especially in the case of LLCs and corporations). You only obtain this "protection" if you both establish the rules of the entity (an operating agreement in the case of an LLC or bylaws in the case of a corporation) AND follow those rules. With LLCs, the members set the rules through their operating agreement. Corporations follow their bylaws, but they are also subject to certain statutory requirements of the state in which they are incorporated and the state in which they do business (if they are different). If you don't follow your rules (even having put them in place), you may still subject yourself and your partners to personal liability. The co-mingling of personal and business accounts and expenses, as well as failing to hold annual corporate meetings can lead to a "piercing of the corporate veil" making assets available to creditors who are chasing you for collection including lawsuits filed against your company. Don't overlook the formalities of running your business!

According to Nolo.com, courts might pierce the corporate veil and impose personal liability on officers, directors, shareholders, or members in certain situations. Personal liability may be imposed when there is no real separation between the company and its owners. If the owners fail to maintain a formal legal separation between their business and their personal financial affairs, a court could find that the corporation or LLC is really just a sham (the owners' alter ego) and that the owners are personally operating the business as if the corporation or LLC didn't exist. For instance, if the owner pays personal bills from the business checking account or ignores the legal formalities that a corporation or LLC must follow (for example, by making important corporate or LLC decisions without recording them in minutes of a meeting), a court could decide that the owner isn't entitled to the limited liability that the corporate business structure would ordinarily provide.

Personal liability may also be imposed if the company's actions were wrongful or fraudulent. If the owner(s) recklessly borrowed and lost money, made business deals knowing the business couldn't pay the invoices, or otherwise acted recklessly or dishonestly, a court could find financial fraud was perpetrated and that the limited liability protection shouldn't apply.

And finally, personal liability may be imposed if the company's creditors suffered an unjust cost. If someone who did business with the company is left with unpaid bills or an unpaid court judgment and the above factors are present, a court will try to correct this unfairness by piercing the veil.

Here are the most common factors that courts consider in determining whether to pierce a corporate veil:

•whether the corporation or LLC engaged in fraudulent behavior
•whether the corporation or LLC failed to follow corporate formalities
•whether the corporation or LLC was inadequately capitalized (if the corporation never had enough funds to operate, it was not really a separate entity that could stand on its own), and
•whether one person or a small group of closely related people were in complete control of the corporation or LLC.

Some corporations and LLCs are especially vulnerable when these factors are considered, simply because of their size and business practices. Closely held companies are more susceptible to losing limited liability status than large, publicly traded corporations. There are several reasons for this.

Small corporations are less likely than their larger counterparts to observe corporate formalities, which makes them more vulnerable to a piercing of their corporate veil. To avoid trouble, it's best to play it safe. It's important for small corporations and LLCs to comply with the rules governing formation and maintenance of a corporation:

- hold annual meetings of directors and shareholders or members.
- keep accurate, detailed records (called "minutes") of important decisions that are made at the meetings.
- adopt company bylaws, and
- make sure that officers and agents abide by those bylaws.

Small business owners may be more likely than their larger counterparts to co-mingle their personal assets with those of the corporation or LLC. For example, some small business owners divert corporate assets for their own personal use by writing a check from the company account to make a payment on a personal mortgage — or by depositing a check made payable to the corporation into the owner's personal bank account. This is called "co-mingling of assets." To avoid trouble, the corporation should maintain its own bank account and the owner should never use the company account for personal use or deposit checks payable to the company in a personal account.

Just know that "piercing" of a corporation and creating personal liability on its owners, is generally an "equitable" remedy, designed to provide fairness to the claimant(s) and "right" a wrong in the opinion of the court. Basically, you should not hide behind your company to avoid obligations and liabilities, purposefully or fraudulently. If your intentions are genuine and honorable, not following corporate formalities might lead a court to conclude otherwise.

Chapter Ten
Failing To Sign Noncompete, Non-Solicitation And Nondisclosure Agreements With Employees And Contractors

We often have ideas and casually mention them to people. We might have someone who starts to work for us, especially during the early days of our business, and they learn the process of running the business, who its customers are, employees, vendors, suppliers, etc. But as you work out your idea, present it to others and allow persons to start working for you, it is very important to protect yourself and your business from theft – the theft of your ideas, customers, employees, contacts, etc.

When discussing your idea, you should always have such person(s) sign a "non-disclosure" agreement. When employees start working, they should sign non-compete, non-solicitation and non-disclosure agreements that, in the very least, prevent them from stealing clients and customers and moving down the street to become your competition.

Non-Disclosure Agreements: More specifically, a non-disclosure agreement (NDA), is a contract between two or more parties whereby one party is disclosing proprietary information about a product, service or process for the purpose of having the other party(ies), the "receiving" party, review and evaluate your idea, product or service. It protects you from the receiver taking your concept and profiting from it on their own. Most importantly, this agreement shows that it was your idea, and the receiver is acknowledging that.

Non-Competes & Non-Solicitations: Depending on your industry and type of business, you might ask employees and other people you do business with to agree not to compete with your company nor solicit ("steal away") customers, employees, vendors, etc. Often, these types of agreements should be signed prior to starting employment, but some states such as New Jersey, even enforce non-competes as an agreement between the parties for "continued" employment. Other states however, specifically as of 2021 Washington, D.C., California, North Dakota and Oklahoma ban the use of employer/employee non-competition agreements in most circumstances. Again, another reason for seeking competent local legal counsel.

At the very least, you should always use non-solicitation agreements where appropriate to keep employees who leave your company and others you do business with from luring away customers and other employees.

While these agreements may be limited in scope by local law or court rulings, they should at least cover a 5-mile radius for a period of up to 2 years. This may also vary from industry to industry. It might be reasonable for someone to be restricted from opening their own retail store in the vicinity for a period of 2 years but restricting a barber from working locally for that long a period of time might be too broad and over-reaching. These agreements should also be in writing and signed correctly or they may not hold up in court or in an action to prevent another employer from hiring your person. Generally speaking, while you can restrict a former employee from competing directly with you, many states' laws will not allow you to prevent him or her from working in their chosen profession or trade. Therefore, these agreements cannot be overly restrictive, or the courts will not uphold them. Sometimes the courts will "blue pencil" the agreement and reduce the restrictions and in other instances, the agreement will be thrown out altogether.

The seminal decision was handed down by the New Jersey Supreme Court in Solari Industries, Inc. v. Malady, 55 NJ 571 (1970). In that case, which somewhat modified prior rulings, the court favored the idea of modifying the agreement unless it was so unreasonable and egregious. The prior appellate division case of Hudson Foam Latex Products, Inc. v. Aiken, 82 NJ Super 508 (1964) favored discarding agreements that were so unreasonable and over-reaching as to give employers an unfair advantage over employees with seemingly limited resources. If you're an employee with limited resources, it may be too costly to challenge. Therefore, more often than not, these agreements are completely discarded. If you plan to enforce such an agreement, make sure you have presented it to the prospective or current employee, encourage them to have it reviewed by an attorney and have them sign and date it. The bottom line: never, never, ever draft these agreements on your own – get competent legal advice and guidance.

SIDEBAR
Protecting Your IP ("Intellectual Property")

As part and parcel to protecting your business from employees and others stealing your ideas, as well as customers and vendor relationships from creating their own competing businesses, it is important to protect all the intellectual property you have created through all your hard work and ingenuity. The question, when it comes to intellectual property, is whether you need to sue or you get sued by someone else. You want to stay on the right side of the law when it comes to issues of possible infringement on someone else's rights. Conversely, you need to be vigilant to protect your own creations. After all, you have made an investment in them. After a candid conversation with experienced trademark and patent attorney Robert Drolet of Bailey Duquette P.C. out of Fort Lauderdale, Florida, we offer you the information you need to know about this subject in order to avoid an unnecessary lawsuit.

Let's first look at the basics. As a business owner, you have a website, you may have a logo, you have a name. You've heard about trademarks and patents. Maybe you even have an invention. You may be wondering what kind of protection does having a trademark really give you? Can I or should I even trademark as a small business owner? What should I trademark? How do I protect my intellectual property from my employees? If somebody leaves my company, how do I prevent them from stealing my intellectual property?

We'll start with trademarks because small business owners often want to trademark their business's name. Does it make sense all the time? Our expert says a resounding "yes." Why? Most intellectual property rights, with the exception of copyright, come from first to file. That means timing is everything when protecting your rights. Let's look at an example of how the statutes are written for trademarks. Let's say you decide after a focus study group, that your name is exactly what you want to capture for your podcast, but maybe you're not using it today. Nonetheless, you file today, protecting that name, the logo and whatever you want to identify your source.

There are different ways to file called "filing bases". One method is when you're already in commerce and the other is commonly known as "intent to use". Here's why it's important. With *intent to use,* you file it, and assuming it goes through the system, it's going to take about eight months until you get a potentially favorable allowance from the government. Then the trademark office gives you six months grace period in order to go ahead and ask for an extension of time. You can keep on doing that for up to three years. Why is it so important to do that? Let's say you filed today. You file your trademark for whatever brand you want to protect. You keep on asking for extensions of time because you're not quite yet in the marketplace. Let's say two years from today, someone else jumps ahead of you and starts using the name you filed to protect, and they are actually doing business in a related class. The issue involves what is known as the likelihood of confusion. Here's what can happen: this other entity goes into commerce before you and starts using the name. At some point after that, when he starts using it, you get your statement of use because you have already been allowed and your registration priority goes back to when you applied before they did. So that's why it's important. Now you can use a common law protection with respect to putting people on notice that it is your slogan, your brand, when they see it—this is your Mark. We've all seen a superscript ™ that designates this. Once the trademark has actually been granted, you then use the ®.

Keep in mind that trademarks exist for two groups. For one, it protects the merchant for the goodwill that you've developed in your business, your client base and recognition of your product. It also serves to protect the public because without someone policing and being able to say that's too similar, you'd have a lot of copycats—a lot of people trying to put something on the market that might be so similar to yours that could cause confusion. Conversely, from your point of view as a business owner, you need to be aware of others' trademarks and avoid creating something that is too similar, which would expose you to potential litigation for infringing on another party's marks.

With a business name, if you try to get an LLC with a name that's already in use, you can use a similar name if it's spelled differently. You can also have an LLC with the same name in another jurisdiction. Similarly, remember when the craze with domain names occurred. Everyone was snatching up and misspelling domain names. That doesn't work with trademarks. If it sounds like it, it looks like it graphically and likely shows confusion with the consumer base it's not going to be allowed.

Show Me the Money

Now, what about enforcement? If I'm a small business, unlike IBM® or Microsoft®, I don't have a lot of money. Big companies have a lot of value behind their brand name, and they can afford to defend any infringement. There was, for example, a company that was called M-Y-CRO-soft. As you can imagine, they got shut down right away. But as a small business owner, I file for a trademark, and somebody starts using my name. Isn't it difficult to enforce and expensive? Doesn't that give the larger companies more of an upper hand? Our expert Rob Drolet says yes, as a general rule. Is there anything you need to do to protect your trademark? They're always going to have the upper hand. That being said, though, it's not too expensive just to get started. Once you find someone in your role in the marketplace that is similar to something that you've already registered, you can just issue a simple cease and desist letter. However, our expert advises *not to put it on the record*. You communicate with that entity directly. Just pick up the phone, have a discussion with the other entity. Tell them you don't think this is right but try to get some common ground between you and the other entity. It's not expensive to do the cease-and-desist letter. Litigation, on the other hand, does become expensive.

Let's pause for a moment to differentiate between trademarks and copyrights. They are not the same. They are used differently and provide different types of protection. While you can't actually copyright an idea, you can copyright the physical expression of an idea. Where trademarks protect your identifying indicia, such as your logo, copyrights are used to protect actual works, such as a book, an article, a musical composition or a sound or video recording. Although the laws have been revised over the years, they still serve to protect the creators of original works in much the same way they always have. With the advent of the internet, however, major updates were required to provide additional protection. The Digital Millennium Copyright Act of 1998 was signed into law under President Bill Clinton and was passed to implement two 1996 World Intellectual Property Organization (WIPO) treaties: the WIPO Copyright Treaty and the WIPO Performances and Phonograms Treaty. This law goes a long way to secure rights to works published in digital formats and proliferated online. Use this link to download an 18-page summary of the act from the US government's copyright website:

https://www.copyright.gov/legislation/dmca.pdf.

It's important to know that you simply cannot appropriate an artist's music as your podcast theme without paying royalties; you cannot reproduce your favorite painting as the background for your website—in fact, you cannot even quote song lyrics in your blog without permission—unless the material has fallen into the public domain. The original copyright law provided for 28 years of protection, renewable once for a total of 56 years. The current copyright law allows for 75 years of protection. However, it is not renewable.

So, inasmuch as you want to stay on the right side of the law and not infringe on anyone else, you also want to know how to protect your own intellectual property, right? Well, it's actually pretty simple. Technically, under the current copyright law, as long as you make the work available to the public with the proper notice: ©2021 Your Name, it is protected. However, we recommend you register the work in order to have proof that you created the work and when, in the event you need to defend against an infringement. Yes, essentially the law passes the burden onto the creator to prove ownership. It's a simple online process to register through the Library of Congress.

https://www.copyright.gov/registration/

So, what exactly are your rights under copyright law? A lot of times there'll be photographers from all over the world, photographing a president. It can almost be the same identical shot but taken by a different photographer. Each one of those photographers has copyright protection of their own photos. Just because it looks the same doesn't mean anything. It's an author's manifestation of something. It could be a statue. It could be a song. It could be anything. They want to protect the IP, the author's creation of works of art. If you're a painter, you're a songwriter, you're an author and you write a book, you should get protection the minute the ink hits the paper, and you then publish it for other people to read. People go and they pitch a movie, they pitch a book to some publisher or a film to a studio and the movie shows up and then they say, wait a minute that was my idea. You do get protection of the law, but your work has to be registered. If I discover that someone's infringing on me and I have proof that I wrote this book 10 years ago, I can then go register it now. Can you go backwards retroactively? Just know this. Damages can only be collected if in fact the work has been registered prior to someone else's use. So, if I had registered a movie script, it got stolen, the film studio made $300 million. I'd have no case. You would have to litigate it. You have to prove that it was stolen. It was yours. You made it first. Because again, the copyright exists as soon as it's made, you have the right to sue them; you just don't have any statutory damages.

We briefly mentioned website creation. This is an especially sticky area for many small businesses, so let's take a deeper dive as it relates to copyrights and your strict liability and exposure to a possible lawsuit. There are a lot of people that set up websites and they start picking material to use—I'll take this from here; oh, this is a good picture of Home Depot. Then they get letters from Getty Images. Just so you know, the statutory damages can range up to $150,000 in some cases. Let's say I hire you to do my website and go on the assumption that you're using pictures that are legal to use and that are free to use. Then I get a cease-and-desist letter. Am I still liable? Do I now have to sue you because you're creating my website?

"Nothing comes onto your website that someone else owns a copyright on."

That's the third-party defendant practice. You're still on the hook because it's yours; you depended upon them. When you are creating all of your website and pages, you have to look to see whether or not every website has the legal entity name, the year, and either copyright or circle C. Be aware that in social property litigation, there's a multiplier. As soon as you can prove willful misconduct, the gloves are off. That's when the jury and the judge can apply the seven factors test to see whether or not they can go up to the highest statutory cap of $50,000 per infringement. Have your website designer sign something stating that all things are either their personal creation or they're open source. It could be considered "work for hire" because you're hiring them to do the design for you. You want to make sure you own it and that everything's covered so nothing comes onto your website that someone else owns a copyright on.

Just as a point of interest, the founding fathers envisioned the need to protect literary and other works. The basis for it is actually right in our constitution, Article One, Section Eight, Clause Eight. It grants Congress the enumerated power "To promote the progress of science and useful arts, by securing for limited times to authors and inventors the exclusive right to their respective writings and discoveries". At the onset of the formation of The United States as its own country, all the brain trust and the new technology existed in

Europe. They wanted to attract people to come over here in the States with their know-how to go ahead and set up an infrastructure. That was one of the things the founding fathers designated as very important in order to have a sustainable economy and sustainable growth.

As with anything in business, however, where there's a will, there's a way—to try to beat the system since it can be expensive to defend trademarks and copyrights. As we indicated, you have to prove damages and litigation can become costly. The offended party needs to prove that the work is substantially similar to theirs and that the defendant could reasonably have been exposed to your work. However, if you registered your creation first, you have the presumption of superior rights. The other party has to actually litigate, and *they* have the burden of proving that they were first in commerce, they're first to use and that their rights are superior to yours.

Let's get into the weeds for a moment. Suppose you have been accused of infringing upon someone's trademark. While you may think that the words used are widely pervasive in the language and therefore not protectable, the other party may claim either tarnishing or dilution. In tarnishing, they are claiming that you're taking their mark and you're doing something nefarious or something that is obscene to society. With dilution, they are claiming that you're actually siphoning off some of their client base due to likely confusion. (Remember the film *Coming to America?* McDonald's would not allow a competing hamburger restaurant to name itself "McDowell's" and use similar logo and signage colors.)

How do you combat that accusation? You look at what's registered; find how many registrations there are with the word in question. Focus on the ones that are in related classes of goods and services. For instance, if it's two different distinct classifications, there's no likely confusion, then they'll allow the same word being used. For instance, Delta® faucets has a registration and you've got Delta® airlines. Someone that's shopping for faucets is not going to be confused with the Delta airline registration. It's with those services or goods that are so closely related that potentially there could be confusion by the consumer in the same or similar marketplace.

While most of the cases that go to litigation are for large companies where the damages claimed could be substantial, for smaller businesses it's worth the nominal investment to file for trademarks and to register for copyrights in order to discourage possible infringement. Patents, on the other hand, are more expensive to file as well as to defend but may be worth it if your company's revenue is derived from your invention or proprietary process. The bottom line: you don't want to be on the receiving end of a lawsuit for infringing on someone else's intellectual property, due to the cost of defending yourself.

The Secret Sauce

Another category of protection involves what we refer to as trade secrets. For example, something like the formula for Coca-Cola® or the recipe for KFC remains under lock and key with only a select few people knowing it or having access to it. So, why don't they patent it? Because when you file for a patent, in exchange for your right to exclusivity for a period of 20 years you have to make your information public. How do you protect those? It's a really tricky thing. You have to have internal procedures in place to protect the trade secret from being known by anyone who doesn't have the need to know. You have to create silos to keep the information restricted. For example, the general manager of a KFC franchise is not going to know the secret of the recipe. It's pre-made and there's no ingredients listed on there. In addition, the people at the factory making the KFC are not going to know everything—just their part, so there are essentially firewalls. Trade secrets can be protected only through litigation. All your employees need to be bound by nondisclosure/noncompete agreements.

With non-competes and NDA's, you don't want to have a 15-page document. It's not going to be upheld. It's probably going to be considered overreaching and possibly ambiguous. In the natural course of things, employees do go from company to company, so even customer lists must be protected. It's also wise to have your vendors sign NDA's. Anybody who has access to the information. With trade secrets, as part of the litigation, you want to be able to show, this is our trade secret and look at the things we've done in our business to protect our secrets so you can demonstrate that it's important to the company. On a really hyper local level, when a stylist leaves a hair salon, his or her customers usually want to follow. They have no loyalty to the business— only to the person. If the employee had signed a non-compete, the new employer typically does not want to deal with a possible lawsuit, court costs and may turn away the customer, so there is some power in it.

Once again, in the spirit of this book, if you are the employee leaving your company and seeking to go into business, take heed. You simply cannot walk out the door with your former employer's formulas, secrets and customer lists without risking a lawsuit.

BONUS CHAPTER
What To Do When the Inevitable Happens; You Get Sued

Now that we have given you 10 chapters of what to do in order to stay out of court, just know that despite all of your best efforts, business owners still get sued. In this chapter, we offer the best advice from our friendly counsel, litigator Edward D. Altabet from the law firm of Cohen, Segalias Pallas, Greenhall & Furman, PC in New York. Ed is admitted to practice in both NY and NJ and advises when you should seek representation, when not to and offer his thoughts about settling, since the reality is that nobody really wins when you go to court. To quote Ed, even the guy or gal who "wins" is often upset with his or her attorney. The experience was aggravating, and they spent a lot of money.

Ed quotes a Justice of the Second Circuit who has said he couldn't imagine anything worse than being a litigant. It's scary. You get that piece of paper in the mail, and you don't know what's coming next. Most people's businesses do not involve them getting regularly sued. If it happens, call a lawyer. They'll look at the complaint and they'll know how to get you to the right firm if they don't handle these matters. Basically, if you're getting sued in connection with your business, you need a civil litigator. (Oh, and by the way, as a business owner you cannot represent yourself in court with limited exception—one of these being Small Claims Court.)

Here is the important thing we can't emphasize enough—you're now in a time window once you get served. The exact amount of time you have to answer the complaint depends on the state that you're being sued in. In New York, for example, you have 20 days to respond to a complaint, whereas in New Jersey it's 35 days to respond. You get served with a summons and complaint. The way the law works, if you don't answer it, you'll get a default judgment entered against you. At that point, once somebody gets a judgment, they can go and enforce it against you. If you have involved an attorney, he or she can get you a little bit of an extension—maybe an extra month or two, but you can't just ignore the complaint. If you ignore it, it will get worse. And be sure to be open, upfront and honest with your lawyer. Do NOT leave any details out!

If you get served a lawsuit, seek legal advice immediately.

Suppose you make that mistake: you ignored the complaint and wound up with a judgment against you? Well, attorney Ed has had just that experience. He has had clients come to him afterwards, asking "What do I do with this?" His answer: "I'm not sure there's anything much I can do." When a motion for a default judgment has been filed, at that point, you still have an opportunity to correct it. However, when the proverbial gavel comes down it becomes more difficult."

Do's and Don'ts for You

Where you operate your business may affect which court has jurisdiction, and what laws and rules will affect your case going forward. For example, if you did a one-off transaction in New York, but your business is domiciled in New Jersey, you may not be subject to jurisdiction in New York. This brings us full circle to our earlier chapters, where we discussed the importance of how you set up your business agreements. To reiterate, that's why putting things in writing is important. If ultimately you do have a dispute and it does move to litigation, (and if you had set up the rules with whatever agreement you have with this person) a jurisdiction choice of law, or maybe an arbitration-mediation provision to first try and settle this dispute, could make a difference. Having that in writing, even if you do get sued, becomes important. Then there are the things you *don't* want to put in writing—and should *not* put in writing. You want to put the right things in emails and avoid the wrong things in emails.

"Never put something in writing that you will be afraid to show up on the front page of The New York Times.*"*

For example, consider what you want to do if you are unhappy with the business relationship, you do want to put that in writing—appropriately and politely. In a typical case, a party wasn't happy with a bank's service. However, they did not tell the bank that during the course of the engagement. Which means they didn't give them an opportunity to cure whatever dissatisfaction they had. That weakens the case when the bank makes its claim for fees they feel they are entitled to receive. Conversely, you never ever want to put something in writing that you will be afraid to show up on the front page of "The New York Times." That's a good rule.

In today's world, what constitutes a writing is itself a fun category. Everybody's got their own form, so it's called "the battle of the forms." You can have an offer with an acceptance by email, that's an addressable writing. In certain types of businesses, a lot of people don't have formal contracts. They conduct business on a handshake and then they send out an invoice. The better practice is obviously to have a form agreement that you tweak and tailor for each client or customer, but you're not without remedies even without a written agreement, except possibly with real estate.

What are the Steps in a Civil Lawsuit?

Let's break down just what happens in a litigation. You can subdivide this into four basic stages. There's the pleading stage, where the other party files a complaint. They sue you; you file an answer, or a motion to dismiss. Next, it moves to discovery. Depending on the case, discovery can last anywhere from three to eighteen months. That hinges on how big the case is, how document-intensive it is and how many witnesses there are. Depositions are taken and documents are gathered. There are cases where discovery goes on for years because it's so complex. It depends on how complicated the underlying transaction is that's gone awry. For example, you might need forensic accountants; you might need data specialists. Many factors affect a complex commercial lawsuit.

10 Ways To Get Sued By Anyone And Everyone

Following depositions, you have your pretrial and then finally, if the case does not settle out of court, you have your trial. Here's where it can get tricky. You're never dealing with the question of whether or not a document's admissible until you hit the pretrial and trial stage. Lots of information is going to come out. The "parole evidence" rule basically says where you have an integrated agreement, you can't use it. In other words, you can't use a prior writing to vary the terms of the instrument. You can look to subsequent writings. The course of conduct and course of dealings between the parties could possibly alter the terms of the written agreement. In other words, how you actually deal with people on a day-to-day basis may inadvertently alter the terms of your contract. For example, you might regularly accept payments from a customer 60 to 90 days from invoice, even though the agreement requires payment within 30 days. If you never enforce the actual terms, your acceptance of the late payments becomes an agreed upon change to the written document.

Discovery has two parts to it. Paper discovery, where you ask people for their internal emails from the other side, and [in return] you get asked for your internal emails. Just know that your communications with your lawyer are privileged. And what that means is that nobody can see those communications. However, if you get sued and you turn to your executive vice-president and you write him a note saying something like, "Oh man, we really screwed up there. Delete all these emails", you've created a bit of a problem for yourself! That's a relevant email. Make sure you never delete anything because you're not allowed to destroy evidence. We have a special word for it— "spoliation" of evidence. Remember, today we have the ability to find them using forensic recovery of deleted emails. Don't put it in writing. Have a conference in somebody's office or a phone call. Do not be texting about your thoughts.

Then there are depositions, which are the other side's opportunity to ask questions of the parties to the suit and other witnesses. You have to sit there and get asked a ton of questions and you must answer them. And while the deposition proceeds, a reporter or stenographer is keeping a written record (often electronically these days). The law treats us as if your memory or recollection is perfect. It's very easy to get tripped up in a deposition and then whatever you said, six, eight months, a year, two years later, you're now testifying in trial. You don't even remember what color underwear you're wearing today let alone, what you said two years ago in the deposition. This is why you probably should review your deposition before you testify. That's also why things need to be in writing (kind of the theme of this entire book!). It becomes easy for the other lawyer to trip you up and say, wait a second. You didn't say that two years ago, you said this. Now you look like a liar because it's a dispute about the facts. When facts are unclear or in dispute, it now becomes the jury's (or judge's) responsibility to determine who is telling the truth. No matter whether you're right or wrong, it matters whether you *look like* you don't remember it.

Part of your attorney's job is preparing you and any friendly witnesses who we have access to before their depositions. Your attorney can't tell your story, but he or she can help you tell your story in a way that both reflects best upon you without locking you in. So, we tell people things like you want to avoid using absolutes. If you get asked a question, don't say, "I never do that." Better answers are things like, "I don't, you know, I don't have a recollection of doing that recently. That's not something I would typically [do]." Just answer the question you are asked. Do not volunteer any additional information – it might come back to haunt you in the future. Remember, you can never win a deposition. One reason why: *you* never get to ask a question in a deposition. The best attorney will prepare their clients well for trial, including conducting a videotaped mock opening and mock cross examination. If you look nervous, it definitely reflects to a jury.

Keep in mind that during the course of any litigation, the landscape can change. For instance, you've got a really important document, but the jury is never going to see it because it is ruled inadmissible. That's something to start thinking about. Litigators tend to think about cases in the reverse. A good attorney will start thinking backwards from trial, back through the pleading stages. That's why we try to help guide clients to start thinking about that. One of the things you want to do is to recognize that there are inflection points and off-ramps in every litigation where there's an opportunity to try to settle the case. Settlement is not a litigation strategy. It's a goal. You still have to litigate a case as if you're going to win it and try it. Obviously, everybody wants to try to settle because you have certainty, and you can hopefully reduce costs and expenses. The imposition a lawsuit has on your life and the aggravation that comes with it are debilitating to a business.

Following depositions, pretrial is like setting the rules for the trial. You're going to have what are called *dispositive* motions for summary judgment, to see if you can get the case decided by the judge. And if not, then you're going to have motions *in limine*, which are arguments about what evidence is admissible or not and what the jury instructions look like. If the case still doesn't settle on the courthouse steps, you all show up and you try the case either before a judge or a jury. You'll have basically two opportunities to really make your full case. One is summary judgment, which happens at the end of discovery. Everybody's done, there's been depositions, documents have been exchanged. At that point you put a 25-50 page brief before the court and say, "Judge, these facts aren't in dispute, here's the law. You should decide my way." Judges often don't like to grant summary judgment because they get subject to reversal. Trial courts do not like to upset jury verdicts.

To Settle, or Not to Settle?

"Businesses can handle risk, but they can't handle uncertainty."

Attorney Ed relates that 98% of his cases settle. "In general, most cases do settle. And the reason most cases settle [or] they get decided on summary judgment is that discovery is a painful process." Understand that if there's a real factual issue, it's a crap shoot as to what a jury is going to do. That uncertainty frightens a lot of people. Businesses can handle risk, but they can't handle uncertainty."

Then, there is stubbornness which can manifest when someone believes they want to win on principle. They want their day in court; they want to be able to get up there and tell their story to a jury and they want a jury to vindicate them. To some people, that is more important than getting a million dollars. Yes, principle is a wonderful thing—if you can afford it.

Ultimately, you still don't know what a court is going to do. You still don't know what an arbitrator is necessarily going to do. The crapshoot element is still there. Think about this analogy: no professional basketball game ends in a shutout. We're going to score points, and your opponent is going to score points. The question is, who's going to have the most points at the end of the game? That's also how you start thinking about settlement. You have got to do a cost- benefit analysis. How much money am I going to pour into lawyers? How much of my time am I going to pour into this versus what kind of settlement value would range? A good litigator will help you try to make sense of what the case values look like so that you can make some educated guess. Most cases settle because people start seeing what the facts are.

When it comes to small business owners, especially in larger metropolitan areas where attorney fees are higher, it becomes too expensive to hire an attorney to litigate these things. In a commercial setting, a lot of times you cannot represent yourself. You can't represent your own company. You have to get a lawyer, and [when] pursuing smaller amounts that becomes difficult. Lawyers charge what they charge because it takes time to learn the case and to put the story together. What is available to people in those situations is small claims court. If you're owed $3,000 in New Jersey or $5,000 in New York, for example, you can go to court and do it on your own.

In most cases, we are under what we call the American rule, which means everybody pays their own attorney's fees, unless there's either a fee shifting statute for public policy reasons, or there's a contract that allows fee shifting. If you do have a contract, you can put in a prevailing party clause. Before you do, think over whether or not you are more likely to be sued or to be the person suing as to whether you want the provision or not.

You Can Run, But You Can't Hide...Your Assets

It's very important to understand that if somebody gets a judgment against you, you can't transfer assets to evade the judgment. It's called a fraudulent conveyance. You can't move assets around to avoid giving them to a creditor. While there's many ways to shield your assets, you really should do it ahead of time. If you have, and if you then impoverished yourself, it would be an issue, as well.

The End Game

As we indicated earlier, settlement's a goal but it's not a strategy. As an attorney, you still have to maneuver yourself in the litigation to be best positioned, to get the best possible settlement out of it. It's a very frustrating thing to be in litigation and then to not understand, why is the attorney doing this? Because when we leverage the situation, to get to a good settlement, you need a good strategy. That's why settlement is not a strategy; it's a result. Attorney Altabet relates,

"I always come in higher or lower than [where] you want to end up because that's a smarter strategy. You have to play the game and you have to play it to win—even though the goal is to try to get a negotiated resolution. The goal is to get what you want and make the party feel like they got what they wanted."

BONUS CHAPTER
Consider Alternative Dispute Resolution

Taking the Sting Out of Resolving Disputes

If you do find yourself in a business dispute, there are ways to resolve it without costly litigation. We refer to these collectively as "alternative dispute resolution" (ADR), which includes methods like arbitration and mediation. As we have indicated throughout this book, always consider incorporating this language into your agreements up front. It could save you time, money and headaches. We consulted Florida-barred attorney and certified mediator Mark Greenberg, owner of Breakthrough Mediation, on the subject.

In Florida and some other states, they allow nonbinding arbitration whereby you get a decision, but you don't have to abide by it. You can still ask for a trial. It's almost like getting a mock trial where you get some feedback on what your case is about and how believable it is. This can be useful if you just need someone else, like an independent person to interpret how they look at it.

The biggest and best alternative to going into court is to settle it beforehand and make that business decision to evaluate it and work it out before you invest time and money. If you are going to court, depending on the size of the dispute, your attorney's fees could easily be higher than the amount you are fighting over. Evaluate beforehand the time and the aggravation that court takes out of you because you are on someone else's schedule—the judge's.

First, as part of avoiding going to court, you can arrange a mediation before filing a lawsuit. It is often voluntary. Mediation is not something that the court always forces you to do. You can agree to do it before a lawsuit is even filed. The courts love it. They will almost always enforce it because judges are evaluated on how many cases they can clear and resolve.

The other form of ADR would be arbitration, which differs in a few ways. The key differences are, as an arbitrator you are making a decision, whereas a mediator just kind of nudges and encourages, but can't force the parties. So as the arbitrator, you are like the judge and jury together. There are two ways to do it. You can agree to mediate. If it doesn't work, that mediator can then become an arbitrator and make the decision. The problem with that is mediation is confidential and you might reveal something in mediation that you wouldn't necessarily volunteer in a trial or arbitration. You can't ask somebody to erase their memory. The flip side is you can do an arbitration first where that arbitrator/mediator writes down his or her decision, puts it in a sealed envelope and then mediates it. If the parties can't settle it, then here's the award. Generally, though, it's better to have a separate mediator and arbitrator.

In some cases, arbitrations can be complete alternatives. Many contracts will say you waive your right to go to court and a jury trial and agree to arbitration under the rules of the American Arbitration Association. You don't go to court, you go to arbitration, and the court's rule is limited to basically ordering you to arbitration and enforcing any award. If there's no judgment and nobody pays it, then you must have the court order it, be enforced and go and have the sheriff seize assets. If you have an arbitrator rule, the advantage is that it doesn't go public. It's private.

If you are having a dispute with somebody in a business situation, how do you start the mediation process? There are two ways to have a mediator chosen. Ninety-nine percent (99%) of the time, everybody involved agrees on the choice of a mediator. They reach out to the mediator, coordinate a time for the mediation and then go through the mediation process. The key part of mediation is the decision makers have to be there. You can't just send your attorney. The principals need to be there who can make decisions, write checks and bind the corporation. With multiple partners, you can delegate to one partner, but all have to agree that if that partner agrees they are on the hook. Generally, everybody meets together in one room. Usually, you do it at one of the attorney's offices. After you start in the general session, you then separate into your own rooms and the mediator then walks back and forth between the different rooms and conveys offers to settle the dispute, ask questions, regulates information and tries to find a way to push everyone into the middle to get it done. The mediator has to remain neutral. The key part of mediation is that it's confidential. What is said in mediation can never be used in court. You can make concessions at mediation that will never be heard in court.

What about evidence requirements? You can't force the other party to bring it to mediation. You can let the mediator know you can't really make an informed decision without this piece of information. The mediator can say you are entitled to get it, and suggest they provide it, but the mediator can't give an opinion on the evidence.

Mediation is generally less expensive than litigating. What does a typical mediation run in terms of fees? First, you are going to split the fees with the other side. It depends on how expensive the mediator is. Mediators charge anywhere from $150 an hour to $800 an hour to $10,000 a day, flat rate plus airfare. Like anything else, it's supply and demand; the more popular the mediator is, the more he or she can charge. but it's generally less expensive than going to court. However, consider that you are splitting the mediation fees and you have to pay your attorney. Mediation will last anywhere from four hours to several days, depending on the type of business disputes because there may be more transactions to unwind. There are more complications sometimes during mediation because you need various pieces of information, or accountants or attorneys have to review it. Mediation can be ongoing; there's no time limit.

"With a court trial, you spend a lot of money to get the same result you could have worked out."

The problem with going to court is that it's going to take two years to get a trial date, realistically—and in some states, even longer. Here is the bottom line: a trial is going to guarantee somebody wins or loses, or even if a jury or a judge kind of splits the baby in some fashion, you are going to spend a lot of money to get that same result that you could have worked out.

With two businesses that may need to work together in the future, settling that dispute, having a chance to shake hands, maybe even air their grievances has a tremendous benefit. Sometimes we will kick the attorneys and the mediator out of the room. The disputing parties may sit in a room and start working things out, but that can only happen once they each had a chance to kind of vent and perhaps grasp that the other side didn't really mean to hurt them in whatever way they perceive they had been hurt. Mediation allows you to agree to things that a court can't order. You get a settlement, and you can put things in a contract; confidentiality, for example. It can include things like non-disparagement, payment terms over a period of time, non-competes that maybe can be agreed upon that a court wouldn't necessarily be able to order.

Let's take a look at the actual process of how mediation works. In an ideal world, the parties will send us summaries that detail what the issues are and copies of any contracts. If there is case law that might pertain to this, the mediator will want to know about it. The mediator will go through the process to facilitate the parties and hopefully will draft the settlement agreement and get them to sign it. Even if it's very basic, it will indicate that the parties agree on these basic terms that are essential. Then they can formalize it in 10 days. For example, this person is going to pay person B this amount to resolve this dispute. They will pay it in this amount of time. There will be a confidentiality in this settlement, and once the money is received, they will dismiss any lawsuit with prejudice or agree that for this issue they can never file suit.

An important point to note: there is really is no such thing as binding mediation, but if you reach an agreement that's signed, that's an enforceable contract. That's not confidential. It can be shown to a court. Businesspeople inherently understand the time value of money so they will be willing to pay an amount and have it off their desk and not invest hundreds of hours of time on it. It's a distraction when they could be building their business and making a lot more money.

If there was an agreement for arbitration, it will usually say, go to the American Arbitration Association or agree on the certain arbitrator. If they can't agree on one, the court will appoint the arbitrator. On occasion, it's a panel of three—and you are paying for all three people, which tends to balance out a decision. The other advantage of arbitration is you get someone who knows the industry, as opposed to a jury, where you get six people who probably know nothing about a slightly complicated issue. Keep in mind that the more you fight, the more issues there are and the more it's going to cost.

In some cases, such as certain employment disputes, a court has to determine whether there is an enforceable contract, whether there is an enforceable arbitration clause and if that clause covers the particular issue. Most courts have held that if it's unclear, the arbitration panel gets to decide whether it's an arbitrable issue or not.

For most small business owners, in your contracts, you want a paragraph that says you will try to work issues out amicably first and if you cannot work it out, you can go to mediation. Then if you cannot work it out, leave it to whatever you want to do next. However, the main thing for small business is putting in the venue and choice of law clauses. Mediators can generally practice in any state. You don't have to be a lawyer to become a mediator in some states. However, most mediators are attorneys.

During the COVID era, settlement rates have been high, using Zoom for mediation. There is no reason that practice can't continue if people agree. It eliminates travel, it's easier to set up and they don't have deadlines. Companies' rules only require them to see a representative who has authority, so they can hire somebody locally to sit there and sign documents if that's what it takes. You can see people's reaction. The downside is if they are a little too comfortable, it doesn't have that same sense of urgency sometimes. If the party is separate from their attorney, sometimes the attorney can have a harder time talking sense to their client. With today's technology, at the end of the day, you can use DocuSign. They can sign the agreement electronically. The other downside to not having people physically present, they kind of miss that interaction. When they are physically present in the room, they are focused, whereas the one issue about Zoom is that you can get easily get distracted.

About The Authors

Mitchell C. Beinhaker, Esq. is a business lawyer and estates attorney who runs a solo legal & consulting practice representing business owners, entrepreneurs, executives and professionals. Through his 30+ years of experience, Mitchell has handled business development, marketing, firm management, along with business transactional work for clients of the firm. He has extensive experience with corporate governance, commercial transactions, real estate and risk analysis. Using his years of practical experience, he drafts contracts, negotiates purchases and can manage outside counsel for any corporate situation. For business owners and executives, he creates and implements estate plans, along with succession plans to help companies continue for future generations.

As a transactional attorney, Mitchell has handled the purchase and sale of multi-million-dollar businesses including insurance portfolios, restaurants, and even a small chemical company. In the real estate area, he has handled and coordinated many commercial purchases and sales from contract drafting and due diligence, including all the zoning and environmental review, through the closing of title. His work has involved helping with insurance and risk management as well as legal involvement with construction management projects.

Mitchell spends his practice development efforts networking, attending professional groups and public speaking. He is also the creator and host of his own audio podcast – "The Accidental Entrepreneur" – where he interviews successful businesspeople and professionals who share their knowledge and help you develop your business. Episodes are available on most podcast directories including Apple® Podcasts, Google® Podcasts, Amazon® Music, and Spotify®. You can follow them on social media including Facebook and LinkedIn.

Mitchell is a graduate of Cornell University ('89) and received his law degree (JD) from New York Law School in 1992. He was a tax intern with Internal Revenue during law school and is admitted to practice in the several states in the New York metropolitan area and practices nationally for federal tax planning matters. He was awarded the Chartered Life Underwriter (CLU) degree from The American College in 1998.

You can follow him on social media: Facebook, LinkedIn, Twitter, Instagram & YouTube.

Barry H. Cohen is the author of the acclaimed book *10 Ways to Screw Up an Ad Campaign* (Simon & Schuster/Adams Media) and co-author of *Startup Smarts* (Simon & Schuster/Adams Media). He is also the co-author of the novel *Comin'Home*, and author of the *Soul Switchers* series of novels.

Mr. Cohen has helped over two dozen other authors launch their publishing projects. His professional career in advertising and public relations dates back to 1979, when he began working in broadcast advertising, eventually transitioning to the ad agency/PR firm environment. He has been a contributor and a columnist to business and trade publications including *Radio Ink, Radio & Records* and *New Jersey Business*. In addition, he has spoken at trade shows and conferences including the Radio Advertising Bureau's annual sales conference, the Natural Products Expo East, the Concert Industry Consortium and a host of others.

Barry holds a bachelor's degree in English *cum laude* from Kean University and has received numerous awards including the Silver Microphone Award, a Leo Award from the Association of Graphic Communicators, Awards of Excellence from the Advertising Club of NJ, to name a few. He has served on the boards of the Kean University Alumni Association and the Advertising Club of NJ. He and his wife have rescued four dogs from the same shelter over the years.

Thank you for reading.

Please review this book. Reviews
help others find Absolutely Amazing eBooks and
inspire us to keep providing these marvelous tales.
If you would like to be put on our email list
to receive updates on new releases,
contests, and promotions, please go to
AbsolutelyAmazingEbooks.com and sign up.

AbsolutelyAmazingeBooks.com
or AA-eBooks.com

For sales, editorial information, subsidiary rights information
or a catalog, please write or phone or e-mail
AbsolutelyAmazingEbooks
Manhanset House
Shelter Island Hts., New York 11965-0342, US
Tel: 212-427-7139
www.AbsolutelyAmazingEbooks.com
bricktower@aol.com
www.IngramContent.com

For sales in the UK and Europe please contact our distributor,
Gazelle Book Services
White Cross Mills
Lancaster, LA1 4XS, UK
Tel: (01524) 68765 Fax: (01524) 63232
email: jacky@gazellebooks.co.uk